Praise For

UNTIL THE BRIGHTER TOMORROW

"A modern-day rags-to-riches story, this book inspires, strengthens, and gives you the determination to strive for all things possible and succeed."

—Michelle Taylor-Jones, CEO, The Taylor Group

"I'm a picky reader, but there is nothing I didn't love about this brutally honest book—the story, the cover, the title, even the typeface. When you devour this masterfully written memoir, you will fall in love with the author as I have. Though I suggested to Valerie long ago that she write her crushing story so the world could learn her lessons, I had no idea how adroit she was with pen and paper. The narrative, insights, and prescriptive dialogue will educate, inspire, and empower you. *Until the Brighter Tomorrow* is simply a book to love and a must-read for those who are serious about navigating life's tragedies to lead a fulfilling life. My heartfelt thanks goes out to Valerie for providing us all a clear way to manifest our destiny. Don't miss this important gem."

—George C. Fraser
Author, *Success Runs in Our Race* and *Click*

"What an incredible story! Women everywhere suffer through many of these same life challenges but often carry the burdens of shame and guilt, sometimes losing their sense of self altogether. *Until the Brighter Tomorrow* is an inspiring must-read—a raw, authentic account that reminds us of the power of courage, strength, and perseverance."

—Carol Evans
President, Working Mother Media

"All I can say is WOW!—this memoir reads like a novel. Although I have heard many parts of Valerie's story before, I continue to be captivated and inspired."

—Marsha Haygood, Co-author, *The Little Black Book of Success: Laws of Leadership for Black Women*

"Our environment shapes us but doesn't define us. Valerie took her adversity and through hard work and vision, became an outstanding servant leader who made and continues to make a significant difference in the lives of others."

—Audra Bohannon
Senior Partner, Korn-Ferry International

"Stories of personal tragedy are often too painful to speak about openly, and even more painful to publish for the world to read. But Valerie's courage in sharing her story gives hope to readers of any age or background who have suffered loss, extreme adversity, or emotional heartbreak, illustrating for them that tenacity and faith are the antidote for despair, even when brighter days seem impossible. An incredible story definitely worth devouring."

—Sheila Robinson
Publisher & CEO, Diversity Woman magazine

"Valerie has an incredibly giving spirit, and this book is a testament to who she is and her commitment to helping people push past life's adversities, even in the midst of their seemingly darkest moments. She is a remarkable business coach, and this book is an amazing personal tool and gift."

—Cheryl B. Walker-Robertson
President & CEO, Protocol International

"*Until the Brighter Tomorrow* is an absolute must-read. This inspirational true story has transformed my interpretation of difficult events endured at any age and outside of one's control, and is a testament to the power, love, and thought in each of Valerie's words, captivating and motivating her readers to believe that ANYTHING is possible."

—Vera S.
Recent college grad and survivor of family suicide

UNTIL

the

BRIGHTER

TOMORROW

ISBN: 978-0-9905193-1-7

Published by Elloree Press, New York.

Cover photo: Dunbar Apartments, New York City. Courtesy Wikimedia Commons; author, Beyond My Ken.

Editing and book design by Stacey Aaronson

Printed in the United States of America

UNTIL

the

BRIGHTER

TOMORROW

—◆—

ONE WOMAN'S
COURAGEOUS CLIMB *from*
the PROJECTS *to the* PODIUM

VALERIE IRICK RAINFORD

ELLOREE PRESS

NEW YORK, USA

In memory of my mom,
a woman of incredible strength.

*D*edicated to my daughters,
Avaree and Alyssa.

Let my story be full of lessons and inspiration for you
of the importance of never giving up.

*A*nd THANK YOU to my husband
and lifelong partner Tony
for standing by me through this journey.

I love you all.

Mommy

ACKNOWLEDGMENTS

There are so many people to thank for helping me not only see the value of telling my story out loud, but also of penning it in the form of a book to help those who are struggling to find their strength and purpose amidst a life of adversity.

I am who I am because of many people to whom I owe my success and tremendous gratitude. To my beloved mother, for instilling in me the value of hard work and for teaching me that I could be anything I put my mind to—despite her inability to see a way of achieving more for herself.

To my grandmother, who taught me the power of faith and resilience, and my dad and brother, Ankie, who exemplified how to enjoy life despite your circumstances. I am grateful that they each passed on these gifts to me before leaving this earth. I am each of them.

I am equally blessed to have a wonderful cheerleading squad surrounding me who encourage my every dream ...

To my big brother Jay, who is my longest running champion. I understand that my telling our story is hard for you but appreciate your supporting me in doing so anyway. To my biggest supporters, my daughters Avaree and Alyssa, the pride you show in this work I am determined to do fuels me even more. And then there's the anchor to my cheering squad—the person who has stood at the center bringing support and gentle encouragement for thirty years—my wonderful husband, Tony. I am so grateful for you.

The idea for telling my story is credited to George Fraser, the author of *Success Runs in Our Race* and *Click*. While my motivation for finally completing it is the result of a chance meeting with another great author and transformation genius, Lisa Nichols—contributor to the book and movie *The Secret*—both of these giants were instrumental in encouraging me to share my story with the world.

Lisa Nichols and her colleague Nicole Roberts Jones are credited with connecting me with my first book editor, the "Words Lady," Marlene Oulton, who helped me draw out the raw emotion in the story so readers would experience the journey with me. God then blessed me to discover Stacey Aaronson, also known as "The Book Doctor," the genius who put the finishing touches on my story, title, and cover design. If it weren't for Stacey, it would have been another five years before getting this precious gift into your hands.

There are many more family, friends, mentors, and mentees who encouraged me along the long journey of birthing this baby—too many to name here. But I would like to offer a special thank you to the following few who committed their time to reading and contributing to various drafts along the way: Marsha Haygood, Michelle Taylor-Jones, Milca Esdaille, Donna Cuomo, and Nancy Andre.

I am grateful for you all.

CONTENTS

THE PAIN

GRIEVING AND HEALING

THE NEXT CHAPTER

THE PAIN

I

— · —

IS THAT YOUR MOTHER?

— · —

IT STARTED AS A pleasant Sunday morning in September of 1984. We were newlyweds in our new, tiny apartment overlooking the Hudson River in Yonkers. My husband, Tony, and I had both grown up in the Bronx, and now here we were, barely adults, breaking out on our own to start living as a couple. Life was good, although the months preceding had been tough. I had finished my sophomore year at Fordham University in the Bronx and worked part-time as a bank teller while I planned our wedding; Tony had worked the night shift as a coupon clerk in New York City. Consequently, we didn't see each other much before our wedding day.

Our blessed event was attended by 250 family members, friends, and work colleagues from both sides. My brother Jay came from South Carolina with his family, and both of his children were in the wedding party. My parents helped me buy the beautiful white wedding gown I wore as I walked down the aisle at St. Luke's Episcopal Church in the Bronx; the reception followed in the church hall down in the basement. Tony's dad, who worked as a mechanic at the Rolls Royce Carriage House in New York City, arranged for us to wrap up the day in style by driving away in a vintage Rolls Royce.

It was a grand wedding by anyone's standards, and we were exceedingly happy. What made it even more special was that with the exception of my dress and that fancy car, almost every dime of the wedding had been paid for with the money Tony and I had saved over the prior year.

Now settled in our beautiful one-bedroom, made even lovelier with the bedroom and living room sets our parents had given us as wedding gifts and a spectacular river view, we knew we would struggle financially. I still worked only part-time as a bank teller with student loans funding my education, but we were in love and that's all that mattered.

We had mapped out our future living expenses before the wedding—a bit burdened with unexpected credit card debt and no savings to fall back on in case of emergencies —hoping that the monetary gifts we would receive would help us get back on track. When we tore through the envelopes on our wedding night to see how much money our guests had gifted us, however, we discovered that we hadn't found the proverbial pot of gold. In fact, we received just enough to take a little spending money on our honeymoon to the Bahamas. We shared a humble laugh over our dashed expectations and felt grateful nonetheless.

Nassau was lovely. It was my first time traveling outside of the United States. Tony was born in England and had spent a good part of his childhood in Jamaica with his maternal grandmother so he knew island life well; I, on the other hand, was thoroughly fascinated. We walked the beach, visited straw markets, took island boat tours, and spent equal time in our hotel room as madly-in-love honeymooners often do. Then, after five days and four nights, it was back to New York—to our little apartment, to school, to work. By mid-September we were settling into the groove of life together—happy to have the hectic wedding-planning days behind us—and I had started my junior year of college.

Then, everything changed.

WE HAD PLANNED TO have a quiet day that September 23rd. We would sometimes travel on weekends from Yonkers down to the Bronx to visit our families, but on that particular Sunday, we decided to stay home. I hadn't seen my mother since the prior week, and because we had only made it a quick trip, I didn't even make it up to her apartment. We talked a bit while standing on the sidewalk outside of her building, and then we rushed over to Tony's family's house for a short visit there. Everyone understood that as newlyweds we were eager to spend time together on weekends since we didn't see each other much during the week, so despite the fact that our previous family visit was only a brief one (and we felt a bit guilty about it), we longed for a day to ourselves.

I woke up feeling great, poised to make my first-ever pot roast for my new husband. When I called my mother to ask her for the recipe, she seemed distant but calmly told me what to do. We finished the call with my telling her that I would phone her later that day to tell her how my meal turned out.

After preparing my roast and being pleased with how it looked simmering in the oven, I tried calling Mom to tell her about my cooking success, but there was no answer. *Maybe she stepped out*, I thought. Oh well, I would try again in a bit.

I was still in the kitchen when the phone rang a short time later. A woman claiming to be a friend of my mother's told me that Mom had been in an accident and was in Jacobi Hospital in the Bronx. I never stopped to ask her name; I just knew I had to get to the hospital right away. We didn't own a car, so Tony called our good friend Michael to come give us a ride.

Driving down to Jacobi, I could only hope that Mom was okay. They hadn't said what happened, so I assumed she had been in a car accident. I had this terrible feeling in the pit of my stomach, but Michael and Tony kept reassuring me that she would be fine. I kept telling myself the same.

We arrived at the hospital, jumped out of Michael's car, and ran through the front doors. The hospital—one of the busiest in New York City—felt empty … or so it seemed. As we slowed from a run to brisk walking, I don't remember seeing a soul in the hallway. The place felt creepy, lonely, and eerily hollow with a strange odor in the air.

As we proceeded down the empty hall, a woman dressed in a white lab coat approached us and asked if I was Valerie. *How did she know who I was?* I wondered, as I nodded in the affirmative. I recognized her voice as that of the woman who had called me on the phone and followed her as she escorted us down the quiet hall to the room where I thought my mom would be.

My cousin Lewis was already in the room and he hugged me. His presence should have alerted me that something was seriously wrong, but everything was happening so fast. They sat me down in a cold metal chair.

"Lewis, what happened?" I asked. "Where's Mom? What's happened to her?"

Lewis looked me straight in the eye. "There was an accident."

"Valerie," the lady in the white lab coat said gently, "I have your brother Jay on the line and he would like to speak with you."

I took the phone. "Jay, what happened?" I practically yelled into the receiver.

I'm sure he must have said more in our brief conversation, but I only recall four distinct words.

"Val, Mommy is dead."

I shook my head in disbelief. "No, no, no …" I said. "That can't be. I just spoke with her. She told me how to make roast beef."

Tony wrapped his arms around me as I realized what my brother said had to be true. I wanted to scream but only tears came instead. Oh my God, how I cried. I have no idea how long it took for that first wave of tears to subside; all I remember is that as the news started to sink in, I brought the phone back up to my ear where my brother was still waiting.

"What happened?" I asked through my tightened throat.

Silence.

I asked again.

"Baby girl," my brother said calmly. "Mommy killed herself."

I stared ahead in shock, afraid to breathe. It made no sense, but I knew my brother wouldn't lie to me so I didn't question him. The only thing I remember with total clarity was sitting in that room, being held by Tony and Lewis, crying until my reservoir of tears ran dry.

When I finally settled down, my brother's voice came through the telephone line again.

"Val, there's something I need for you to do."

I heard my brother take a deep breath.

"One of us needs to identify Mommy's body, and since I can't get there today, we need you to do it."

I don't remember my reaction to his words, nor do I recall any more tears. It was as if my brain had shut down and there was no space for any additional information.

The next thing I recall is standing at a door with a covered window, Tony on one side of me and the lady in the white lab coat on the other. Lewis, I am sure, was somewhere nearby, but I can't remember. I heard the woman say to me that when she pulled back the curtain to the window, I would see my mom, but only from her eyes down to her chin. She explained that the rest of her would be covered.

As she slid the window covering back, I saw Mom's closed eyes. There were no signs of worry on her face. She looked like she was simply sleeping.

"Is that your mom?" the woman asked.

The tears once again began flowing down my cheeks. "Yes," I whispered.

I LATER LEARNED WHY I was not allowed to see her entire face. My mom had placed a gun to her head and pulled the trigger, one month after my wedding day and ten days after my 20th birthday.

2

CAN YOU HEAR ME?

V al, baby, stop crying. Please stop crying. Oh my God, what have I done?!

"Oh my God, she can't hear me. What did I do? What was I thinking? I didn't mean to hurt you. Please don't hate me. I can see you and I can hear you, but you can't hear me. I can hear you sobbing. How could I not have realized how much this would hurt you? I wasn't thinking clearly.

"It's okay, baby girl. Stop screaming so you can hear me. I know this is hard. I didn't mean to cause you this much pain. I need you to stop crying so you can hear me. Val, please baby, listen to me. I need to explain …

"I just couldn't take it anymore. I was so tired of everything, of working three jobs and never getting ahead. Life has just been so hard, one battle after another. I know I've told you that 'trouble don't last always,' but it seems that didn't apply to me lately. I tried to fight through it, but I just didn't have anything left.

"But you're going to be okay. You're in college. That was my dream for you and you did it. You've married a good man. I know he'll take good care of you. Lean on him as you're doing right this moment. He'll help you get through this. Please understand everything I ever did was for you. My life revolved around you. THIS, however, is not about YOU. It was about me, about me being tired of fighting.

"You need to fight for YOU now. Fight through this. You can do this, I know you can. I wish I could change things, but I can't. Don't let this ruin things for you ...

"Oh, how I wish you could hear me ..."

3

FOREVER ETCHED ON MY SOUL

I COULDN'T LOOK ANYMORE through that glass square in the door. The only thing I could do was sob. My sole memory of that moment standing at the morgue window was my screaming and sobbing ... and seeing Mom's closed eyes draped in those white sheets. I didn't need to see the rest of her face. Her eyes in that moment are forever etched on my soul.

The sobs were so intense they felt like they came from deep within. They seemed to never stop, blurring actions for days afterward. I don't remember when my brother Jay arrived in New York from South Carolina for the funeral, but I know he was there. I don't remember making any funeral arrangements either, but I know I must have been involved in the planning.

The wake was held at McCall's Funeral Hall in the Bronx where hoards of people came to pay their respects. I don't know who or how many; I only remember the line of people waiting to hug me—an ongoing stream of obscure faces that seemed like it would never end.

A week later, Mom was memorialized at Brown Chapel church in South Carolina—the church that she and my dad were raised and schooled in—then buried next to my brother Ankie in the Brown Chapel cemetery. She was in an open casket wearing the beautiful pink gown she had worn to my wedding. She looked beautiful in the dress, but I couldn't look at her long without remembering her eyes draped in those white sheets—the ones that covered the damage caused by the single bullet wound to her head.

MY HOME IS FILLED with pictures of my mother, images of her before that dreadful day surrounded me. My wedding album sits on the coffee table in the living room; photos of her are on the wall in the family room. A picture of her in her youth sits on the nightstand in the guest room that would have been hers had she lived. I didn't put that picture there consciously, but I realize now in my writing and reflecting that this room is set up for her as she would have liked it had she ever visited us.

On the wall of the private bathroom is a portrait of an

old woman's hands as she quilts. I found it in a book on black history, clipped it, framed it, and hung it on that wall years ago because it reminded me of my own grandmother who was a talented quilter. That photo soothes me as I know it would have also soothed my mother. But I still can't look at her eyes without remembering how she looked through that single window in the morgue.

4

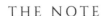

THE NOTE

THE WEEKS, MONTHS, AND even years after Mom's suicide are still a fog to me. In hindsight, likely due to the effects of mental shock, my memories are vague. What I'll never forget, however, is how lost, confused, scared, and terribly guilty I felt.

How could she do this? I thought. *What the hell was she thinking? What could have been so bad? What did I do to contribute to her actions? What could I have done to keep it from happening?*

The first time I went to Mom's apartment after the day she committed suicide, I found the note, perched just inside the front door of her apartment. It was attached to an envelope with my name handwritten on the front.

Val, I'm sorry. I couldn't take it anymore.
Take care of yourself.
I love you.

Inside the envelope was a small life insurance policy, just enough to pay for her funeral. She had left it there specifically for me to find.

Having locked it away in my home safe, I hadn't looked at the note until I was writing this book for fear of reliving the moment I found it. When I finally got up the courage to bring it out, I cried as if that day was happening all over again.

IT ISN'T SURPRISING THAT in addition to all of the other emotions that plagued me during that time, I was also very angry. Ironically, I didn't spend too much time being angry with my mother; perhaps the pain and guilt were too deep. I knew how difficult life had been for her, and I also knew how hard she had always tried. Although I had moments of being angry with her for deserting me, they would be short lived, pushed aside by sadness and guilt. My anger would instead be directed first at me and then at Tony. I believed I had abandoned my mother when she needed me most, that I should have been there for her, that I should have never left home to get married.

It made for a terrible way to start Tony's and my life together. Outward, I was sad and frequently reserved, plagued by my thoughts; inside I was heartbroken and scared, often taking my frustrations out on the man I had just wed. He comforted me during the emotional roller coaster I was on, never realizing that I was sometimes resentful of him for taking me away from her.

My mind was a shambles, making me wonder if I was destined for the same end as my mother. My brother Jay and I actually made a promise after my mother killed herself that we would reach out to each other if we ever felt like killing ourselves too, often wondering if suicide was hereditary. Not only had our mom chosen to end her life this way, but our brother Ankie had taken his life only a few years earlier.

I walked around for a long time pondering if I could ever become so overwhelmed that I would put a gun to my head and pull the trigger. Would death be instantaneous? Would I even be able to make the call to my brother Jay—before I did anything drastic—as I had promised him?

And then I received a call that added a whole new layer to my guilt and emotional pain.

Soon after Mom died, one of her "friends" reached out to me. Miss Ann was supposedly a God-fearing, church-going woman, and she and Mom had been friends for years, having worked together as nurse's aides at Misericordia Hospital in the Bronx.

Miss Ann called to check on me and see how I was doing. We chatted for a bit about how much she missed Mom and what a good friend she had been over the years. Then, toward the end of the call, she said, "Val, did your mother happen to mention that she owed me some money?"

I felt a stab in my already broken heart. I was too

stunned at first to speak, but after a few moments I responded, "No."

"Oh," she went on, "I thought she may have mentioned it to you. Well, as things settle down, please keep me in mind. I could really use it."

I was stunned, not knowing what to say.

Miss Ann broke the silence. "Well, you take care of yourself and that baby."

"Excuse me?"

"You have to be careful in your condition" she said. "You *are* pregnant, aren't you?"

"No, I'm not."

"Oh, we all thought you were pregnant. Isn't that why you got married so early?"

Who the hell was "we all"? I thought, but out of respect didn't ask.

"Miss Ann, I got married because I was in love."

"Oh," was all she could say.

After another awkward pause, she closed the conversation by saying, "Well, okay then. You still take care of yourself and let me know if you come up with any money for me, okay?"

That was the last time I ever heard from Miss Ann, my mother's so-called friend. I never asked the amount my mother owed her, but I knew her well enough to know that it was not a huge sum, plus Miss Ann likely didn't have much excess money to loan anyone in the first place. I also knew that whatever the amount was, it had to trouble Mom to ask for it. I knew that at times she would borrow money from family and friends to make ends meet, but she didn't like to do it and it was always an amount she knew she could pay back.

"If you find yourself having to borrow money from someone," Mom would say, "make sure you always pay them back. You never know when you might need them again."

Miss Ann never called again "to check up on me" or to ask me for the money. Perhaps she realized the absurdity of her call. If the situation was reversed, I am certain that my mother, no matter how bad things were, would never have made such a call to Miss Ann's family.

Despite her apparent lack of common decency, Miss Ann's call laid bare the idea that the lifetime of money struggles Mom experienced had finally overwhelmed her. I often wondered if I should have stayed at home and continued to work and help her pay the bills, or if my moving out caused her breakdown. And though it crossed my mind, I didn't dwell on the question about my being pregnant as that was plain stupid. My mom would have confronted me if she suspected that were the case.

No matter how I tried to reconcile the cause, however, her suicide still didn't make any sense to me. I continued to question whether it was my fault, plagued by persistent guilt. I had an aversion for years to cooking roast beef—or even looking at it in the supermarket—as if it were a bad omen, a glaring symbol of sadness and fear. I even blamed myself for letting her buy that pink dress for my wedding. *How could I have been so thoughtless, so selfish?* I thought. *She couldn't afford that dress!* She had bought it because she wanted me to be happy with how wonderful she looked on my wedding day ... and then we had buried her in it—the most expensive dress she had ever owned.

I carried the guilt for years of all the "what-ifs" I couldn't answer, of how she had sacrificed so much for me and I had let her down, even deserted her. Was the amount she had borrowed from Miss Ann larger than I thought? I wished I would have asked how much it was when Miss Ann called. Now, I would never know.

Ultimately, the guilt overpowered the anger, and to his credit, Tony was wonderfully patient with me. He was always there and incredibly supportive even through my emotional shifts, which was all the more heroic when I realized I wasn't the only one grieving.

Tony and Mom were very close. She would cook for him when he came over to see me, and since they both worked nights, on Saturday mornings after work they would both arrive at the apartment at around the same time for us all to have breakfast together. When we wanted to go out on a date to the movies, she would generously loan him her car. I would often complain that he could borrow the car with nary a question or complaint, but I couldn't take it around the corner. Mom would simply brush off my comments. The truth was, she trusted him with her car—and also with me.

I only remember one occasion when Mom got angry with Tony. We had borrowed her peach-colored Chevy Monte Carlo to go to a track meet, Mom saying that we could take her car as long as we were back by 10:30 p.m. so that she could go to work that night. We left the stadium a little early—and with enough time to get home by our assigned curfew—but soon realized we had rushed into the stadium without taking note of where we parked.

We walked around and around the still-full stadium parking lot to no avail, stunned that we couldn't find a peach-colored car. We then panicked, knowing Mom was going to be upset and would probably never loan us her car again. We thought of calling to let her know we would be late, but that would have meant going back into the stadium to find a pay phone. Besides, how would we explain that we had lost her car?

It wasn't until after midnight when the event was over and the parking lot was nearly empty that we spotted Mom's car. We jumped in and raced home. When we reached the apartment, Mom quickly grabbed the keys as we tried to explain, rushing out of the apartment saying she "couldn't afford to lose her job over our foolishness."

We learned a valuable lesson that night. To this day, we share a chuckle and take a mental note of where we park our car in large parking lots, remembering how panicked we were the night we lost Mom's car for a few hours.

After the incident blew over, Mom continued to loan us—or rather loan *Tony*—her car when we wanted to go out, remaining very supportive of our relationship. I suspect that she was also relieved that night when we arrived home safe and sound.

BELIEVE IT OR NOT, Tony and I have never talked about the details of Mom's suicide. He held me when I needed to be held and let me be quiet when he knew I needed to simply think. My silent anger toward him dissipated over time as I thought about their relationship and how much Mom loved him and supported our being together.

While I'll never know specifically why Mom killed herself, I have come to believe that she would never have done so if it weren't for Tony's presence in my life. She held on and kept fighting until she knew someone else was there to take care of me. I believe she knew that Tony would see me through that terrible time, and he did. She had fought the good fight for years until she had no more fight left, knowing that in leaving me, I would be in good hands.

GRIEVING

AND

HEALING

5

HER CHALLENGING BEGINNING

OM'S CHILDHOOD WAS ONE based on hard manual labor in the cotton fields of Elloree, South Carolina. My maternal grandparents, Otis and Corinne, had six children: three girls and three boys, including my mother Betty. Otis died in 1935 when the youngest of those children, Aunt Flossie, was only one year old and my mother was six. The eldest of the children was my Uncle Junior (Otis Junior) who was fourteen.

Prior to my grandfather's death, my grandparents worked the fields for years on Mr. Houck's land, one of the local white landowners. They earned a living by harvesting his cotton in exchange for pennies a pound, while living in a three-room shack on Mr. Houck's property. Each day, from sunup to sundown, my grandfather and the older children would work the fields harvesting crops on the surrounding land. Only days after the accident in which my grandfather and his horse and buggy were run off the road by a car and he was left to die in a ditch, my grandmother was put out of her home and left homeless with six children.

Mr. Houck's land was intended for sharecropping. Without my grandfather, it would be hard for Grandma to tend the land—and hard for old man Houck to make an income as a result—so he put a lock on the barn where all her tools and equipment were located, leaving my grandmother to fend for herself.

Grandma's parents were long deceased—with her own mother, Winnie, dying years before during the Bubonic Plague of the 1920s—so with nowhere else to turn, my grandmother was forced to live with her mother's sister, Aunt Florence.

Five of the six children picked cotton during harvest season alongside Aunt Florence instead of attending school. Off-season they went to school at the family church, Brown Chapel African-Methodist Episcopal, where three grades were taught basic reading, writing, and arithmetic in a single classroom. Mom went to school during harvest season, and after that worked in the fields full-time for the rest of the year. She never had the opportunity to return to school after the sixth grade.

My grandmother worked hard at various jobs to provide for her children, doing everything she could to earn money—from working the fields to cooking and cleaning houses. She even planted trees for the government's Work Projects Administration (WPA), President Roosevelt's New Deal program of the 1930s. Her children were left to sharecrop with Aunt Florence during the day while she would walk miles each morning to her job to plant trees along South Carolina highways. Whenever I'm back in South Carolina, I can't help but wonder which of the beautiful trees that line the roads were planted there with my grandmother's bare hands almost 100 years ago.

Grandma was a stern matriarch, no doubt concerned about raising her children without a man in the house. My Uncle Junior carried the greatest burden to help his mother raise and feed his siblings, telling tales of picking a little extra cotton that he kept on the side to sell for himself rather than turn it in with his other share-cropping. He would also keep an egg or two when gathering a dozen, or keep a couple of peaches when collecting a full crate. He was even known to steal a chicken or two to make sure all the children had enough to eat. While not an honest living, it was certainly a necessary one under the circumstances. And the girls worked nonstop too. In addition to sharecropping and chopping wood, they were also required to clean house, and wash and iron the family clothes.

This grueling daily scene was my mother's life until she was seventeen. She would often tell me how much she hated that period of her life, and that as she got older, she would look out across the fields at the boys "cropping," searching for the man of her dreams who would take her out of the fields and save her blistered hands.

One day, she got sweet on a "red-skinned" young man by the name of Ed. Edward Irick was four years older, and he had just returned home from a tour in the Navy where he served as a cook on a ship toward the end of World War II. He and his family sharecropped nearby land and also attended the same church and school at Brown Chapel. Soon, he and my mother began courting, and not long after got married on Valentine's Day in 1947, just one month before my mother turned eighteen. Nine months later, Betty and Ed were blessed with a baby boy they named Edward Irick, Jr., who they would nickname "Jay."

Mom's middle sister, Wilhelmina (who they called Bill), gave birth to a son named Lewis one month later. Jay and Lewis grew up as close as brothers, learning how to sharecrop alongside their mothers. They would also learn a bit from our Uncle Junior about survival, cultivating their own stories about skimming peaches off the pickings for the day.

In 1953, six years after my brother Jay was born, my parents were blessed with another son they named Anthony, affectionately referred to as "Ankie."

My mother and father worked tirelessly and eventually fulfilled their wish of moving their family out of the country to nearby Columbia, South Carolina. There, my father—who was also limited by a sixth grade education—was only able to find work as a truck driver and auto mechanic. Always handy, he would often pick up odd jobs working on local homes doing everything from fixing doors to making cabinets. My mother supplemented their income by performing domestic work.

When I entered the world in September of 1964, I joined my family in the first home my parents were able to buy—at 118 Paul Street in the Greenview section of Columbia. My brothers would tell me stories of how much they loved having a new little sister, but how much they hated that Mom made them take me with them whenever they wanted to go out. My brother Jay now jokes about how he eventually got used to taking me with him and even liked it once he realized that I was a "chick magnet." All the girls wanted to be with the cute guy who took such good care of his baby sister.

Because my parents were always working two and three jobs to make ends meet, my brothers provided a lot of my care, including combing and braiding my "mess of hair," according to them. But when Jay left for Vietnam in 1965, Ankie was left to take care of me a lot on his own while our parents worked.

By the time I turned four, my parents divorced. I didn't know the circumstances of their breakup as my parents never talked about it, but my aunt later told me that it was over money. I suspect that it was more than that, but it probably didn't help that they never had enough to make ends meet, making it understandably stressful on their relationship.

When my parents divorced, our family essentially split apart. Jay was still off at war and Dad moved to Connecticut where some of his siblings now lived. Around this time, Ankie's teenaged girlfriend became pregnant and they started living together, so it was mostly Mom and I from then on.

Life became even tougher for Mom after the divorce. She had few options and very little money, but she worked diligently to provide for us. Dad sent what he could, when he could, and wrote letters to keep in touch.

Mom couldn't afford child care, so I started going to work with her when I was five. At the time, she was working as a cook in a drive-in burger joint in Greenview, which wasn't really a "drive-in" or a "drive-thru" as we refer to them today, but rather a walk-up restaurant, very similar to a small, local neighborhood ice cream parlor. It had one small window, and typically one person took the orders, cooked the food, and served the customers. Friday and Saturday nights were the busiest, so those were the times I would help out. I had my own box to stand on to help take the food orders through the window, and after a while, the customers were all familiar faces who knew Mom and me well. They didn't mind that the line chugged along; the cute little girl behind the window always drew their attention.

Mom taught me how to take orders, write them down on a little pad, and even help collect and count money. My fondest memories to this day are the smiling faces that always seemed to be admiring me as I worked, and I liked showing them that I knew how to work hard. What's more, I looked forward to the extra nickel or dime that I was sometimes given for doing a good job.

Though we maintained that routine for a while, things continued to be tough on my mother. Struggling to make ends meet, she eventually migrated up north to New York where her sisters and one brother lived, while I stayed behind in South Carolina with a close friend of my mother's named Aunt Babe (pronounced "Baby") and her family.

Aunt Babe and her husband, Uncle Ed, had four daughters, and they raised me as their fifth child. I did everything with them as if they were my own family, and they never treated me like an outsider. For about a year, it was as if I had four older sisters and no worries. I ate well, had a nice warm bed to sleep in, and a family who loved me. I had everything in the material sense of the word ... but I didn't have my mother.

I would eventually move to New York at the age of six, just in time for first grade. With the help of Aunt Flossie, Mom landed a nurse's aide position working at the same hospital, Misericordia in the Bronx. It was a steady job with meager pay, but Mom was grateful for the opportunity. For a woman with little education, she knew how to get and keep a decent job. She mostly worked as a nurse's aide at night and as a home care attendant for the elderly during the day. Sometimes she cooked and cleaned on the side as well, following in her mother's footsteps, doing what was needed to care for her family.

Once I moved to New York, I was able to see my dad more often. Even though we had to change residences quite a bit—for one reason or another, things just never worked out as planned—he would drive down to the Bronx to pick me up to spend alternate weekends with him in Connecticut. I enjoyed visiting him and getting to know my relatives there. Dad and I would go to the beach or go fishing, and he even took me to the rifle range once when I was about ten years old. I remember everybody scattering when the backfire from the gun scared me and I threw the rifle down on the ground. Needless to say, we never did that again.

I can count at least six different apartments we lived in when I was between the ages of six and twelve before things somewhat settled down. Either the landlord was abusive, there was no heat during the winter, or the place was rodent infested. There was always something wrong. We just couldn't catch a break.

Because we lived in so many places, I also changed schools a lot. Nearly every year I was in a different school —a total of six by the time I got to seventh grade. It was hard to make friends or feel secure with so much instability in my home life, but the one constant was that my mom and I always had each other.

Living paycheck to paycheck, my working and helping out was never an option for me; it was simply expected and never questioned. In fact, when I turned twelve, I got my own job to help Mom with the bills. In the evenings after school, I would sometimes cook our dinner, and every night I would put curlers in Mom's hair as her arms were often too tired for her to put them in herself. She would lie down and fall asleep while I did this—never a night went by that I didn't perform the ritual for her. My grandmother had a similar routine of brushing, braiding, and wrapping her hair each night as well. It's funny what habits we inherit—to this day I can't go to bed without making sure my hair is prepared for the next day.

In caring for my mother's hair each night, I'd nudge her when one side was done so she could turn over in her sleep. I'd then put curlers in the other side of her hair until the job was finished. Sometimes, I would even rub her tired feet with warm rubbing alcohol to help take away the pain. After that, I had a few hours to do my homework while Mom slept before rising at 10 p.m. to get ready for her 11:00 p.m. shift at the hospital.

I'd stay up until Mom left each night in order to secure the locks on the apartment door after she left. There were three deadbolts, and after Mom stepped outside, she wouldn't leave until she heard the click of the locks for each one. She would call me to check in when she arrived at work and then the following morning to wake me up for school.

Mom and I were a team. I knew how tirelessly she worked so I in turn did the same. I never wanted to disappoint her or let her down. When I moved out at nineteen to get married, however, I wasn't thinking about the team my mother and I had become over the years, or how my leaving would affect her. I was madly in love and she seemed happy for me. I selfishly only thought of the new bond I was creating with Tony, but in the aftermath of her suicide, I could only think that I had deserted her. After years of caring for each other, I had walked out on her, and the guilt of having done so weighed me down.

But I knew my mother was a survivor. She had taught me the same work ethic she learned from her own mother, and although I watched her struggle, she wasn't one to get tired of hard work or give in to weakness.

So what did that note she left for me mean? I wondered. *What was she tired of? What couldn't she take anymore?* Maybe she thought she was helping me understand by leaving the note, but it simply left me with more unanswered questions.

6

MOSES

I CONTINUED TO DWELL on memories of our time together for answers to my mother's suicide, and one I couldn't let go was the memory of Moses.

I was around seven years old and had moved to New York the prior year. My mother was working at the hospital and had recently gotten remarried. I was in the second grade and attending P.S. 23 down the street from their apartment near 169th Street and Tinton Avenue in the South Bronx.

Moses didn't pay me any attention and I was grateful. He never talked to me, never even acknowledged me. I wondered if he even knew my name. He wasn't a very nice man, and since he never seemed to want me around, I suspected I was the reason he would always argue with my mother.

My one vivid memory of living in that place was a night when Mom and Moses had another of their many spats. He had been drinking, which he did often, and when he drank, he became argumentative and verbally abusive to my mother. Since Mom was not the kind of person to back down from a fight, she would always stand up to him. The arguments were loud, but they mostly occurred when I was in another room where I could only hear and not see them.

That night, I was in my room when the harsh words began to fly. I stayed in my bed, trying to block out the noise, but when the arguing escalated and my mom screamed, I jumped out of bed to see what was happening. I saw Moses chasing after her, trying to grab her but stumbling in his drunkenness, so I ran out of my room yelling, "Leave my mommy alone! Leave my mommy alone!"

Ignoring my pleas, he kept after her, grabbing at her with one hand while pushing me away with the other. Next thing I knew, he snatched a half-empty beer bottle from a nearby table and hit her over her head with it, smashing the bottle and splattering glass all over the room. Mom stopped screaming and fell to the floor. Moses dropped the broken bottle and ran from the apartment, leaving me crying over my mother's lifeless body, begging her to wake up. I had no idea what to do. I thought he had killed her.

Mom opened her eyes a few moments later and I

hugged her with relief. She told me not to worry and said everything would be okay as she stumbled toward the telephone. She called her brother Paul who came right over.

After Uncle Paul took my mother to the hospital, he took me home with him to spend the rest of the night with his wife and daughter. Throughout that night I lay awake, crying and wondering whether everything was really going to be okay as Mom had promised.

JUST BEFORE DAWN, my uncle returned home with my mother. The doctors had removed the glass from her head, and there was a shaved spot where stitches now resided.

I don't remember if we went back to that apartment, but I do remember Mom sending me back to South Carolina to live with Aunt Babe again, where I finished the last half of second grade.

Moving around so much, I often have to pause and think of which school I attended for which grade. Most kids can look happily back on their school years and friends during that time, but for me, there was simply too much going on to remember every detail.

I do know that by the fourth grade, we were living back up in the northeast Bronx and I was attending P.S. 78. Moses no longer around, though he would occasionally call my mom to ask to get back together—or so I would overhear her telling her sister, my Aunt Bill. Mom didn't take him back and I believe that was because of me. She was resolute to not ever have me see her in that situation again.

The disastrous marriage to Moses was another in a long line of setbacks for my mother. She had male friends after that, but she never remarried. She would always drill into my head, however, the importance of finding a good man and of never letting a man raise his hand to me. She told me to never stay in a relationship that was unhealthy, and to always make sure I had the means to get out of any bad situation if I needed to. She was constantly prescribing the need to be independent, telling me to always be able to take care of myself.

In reflecting back on the Moses period in our lives, the image is reinforced of Mom as a woman of great strength. Being weak was not in her nature or vocabulary. If she was in a bad situation, she would fight through it and eventually get out of it, determined not to repeat the same mistake—and even more determined that *I* not repeat her mistakes either, leaving me with yet another reason why the words she left in her note to me made no sense at all.

7

CAN'T CATCH A BREAK

WHEN I WAS IN fifth grade, we moved into a house on Boller Avenue, a dead-end street right beside the Hutchinson River Parkway in the Bronx. My Aunt Bill helped Mom find the two-bedroom basement unit in the dual-family home (where she and her family lived in the main apartment upstairs), and while we lived there, I attended P.S. 111 on Baychester Avenue. The backyard was part of the infamous swamp that Co-op City is reportedly built on, and my bedroom was at the front of the apartment, while Mom's was toward the back behind the kitchen.

One night while I was asleep, I felt something strange and heavy on my chest. At first, I moved a little and it went away. A short time later when I felt it again, I realized that something was on top of me. I jumped up on my bed and screamed, sending Mom running into my room.

When she turned on the light, a swamp rat nearly the size of a cat was crouched in the corner of my room staring at us. I was petrified and couldn't help but scream while Mom chased the rat out of the room, throwing her bedroom slipper at it as it scampered away.

I don't remember where we slept that night; I only recall being scared and trembling as my mom comforted me and held me tight. We were grateful the rat hadn't bitten me, but it did scare the daylights out of me. Even today, there are nights I startle awake with sweat pouring down my face, trembling at the memory of little feet scampering across my chest.

The next day, Mom had it out with our landlord, Mr. Anderson, which resulted in us packing again. This would be our sixth move in six years.

IN OUR VOLATILE CIRCUMSTANCES, Mom always tried to have a little extra cash on hand for emergencies. Though it never amounted to much, she always stressed the importance of being prepared for unexpected difficulties. Mom would let me know her hiding places "just in case anything ever happened to her," as she drilled into me the importance of saving a little for a rainy day. Frankly, there were a lot of rainy days in my childhood years and there never seemed to be enough money to see us through them, but she held strong to her advice nonetheless.

Mom didn't believe in keeping her money in the bank —her philosophy was to always have a small sum she could get to quickly—so she stashed her savings in creative places where no one would ever be able to find it. In this particular case, her hiding place was in the living room. Back in those days, window curtains had hems at the bottom that were three to four inches tall. Mom had let the seam out at the bottom of one of the curtains and tucked her cash just inside for safety. She was sure that no burglar would ever think to look in a curtain hem, and to her it was safer there than in any bank. To make it even more burglar proof, Mom pushed the sofa up against the window so that her makeshift safe was behind it. In hindsight, it was pretty creative hiding on her part.

As we packed and prepared to move yet again, Mom pulled the sofa away from the window to retrieve her rainy-day stash.

"Oh my God, NO!" she screamed.

I ran into the room to see what had happened. The money was there, or at least pieces of it were. The rats had eaten holes in the bills that Mom had worked so hard to save. With their sharp teeth, they had chewed through the curtain hem, shredding the money beyond repair. Mommy was crushed as I stood there and watched her cry. All she kept saying was "Dear Lord, why can't I catch a break?!"

But Mom was determined to get her baby out of

harm's way, and within a week or so, we moved out of that apartment. I didn't know where she got the money for us to move until recently, when my cousin Lewis told me that Mom "hit the number" and borrowed the rest. Back in those days, an illegal numbers game was run out of the local fish and chip restaurant owned by one of Mom's friends. Apparently her favorite number was drawn soon after the rat incident and she won enough money to help us move.

Mom repeated her oft-quoted phrase as we drove away from that rat-infested apartment: "Don't worry baby, things will get better. Where there's a will, there's a way."

What she didn't know was that I wasn't worried. I trusted Mom to always find a way.

8

———◆•◆———

THE UNFORGETTABLE LESSON

———◆•◆———

LIFE FINALLY STARTED TO settle down for us when I entered junior high school in the seventh grade. It was the first time since coming to New York that we would live in one place for any length of time, and that I would attend a single school for longer than one year. It was also the first time I started to make friends and hang out like other teenagers in the neighborhood on a regular basis.

We lived in a two-bedroom apartment in a four-story walk-up building on the third floor. Hillside Homes on Fish Avenue in the Bronx was an apartment complex with better living conditions than we had ever had. The kitchen and my bedroom window overlooked the street below, facing a row of buildings on the other side identical to ours.

Once again, my Aunt Bill helped us find a new place to live. It was a rent-controlled complex for low-income families. I remember the three of us—Mommy, Aunt Bill, and I—going into the rental office for our initial visit and being turned away. Mom wanted a two-bedroom apartment so that I could have my own room, but she was told that she made too much money to qualify for a one-bedroom and not enough to qualify for a two-bedroom. In addition, she was told that since I was a female child under the age of thirteen, they expected us to sleep together in a one-bedroom apartment—the one she oddly she didn't qualify for.

None of it made any sense. We left the rental office that day disappointed, but Mom was determined not to take no for answer.

The following week, we returned to the rental office and submitted a new application. This time we had two additions that would help us qualify for the larger apartment. The first was a letter written by my dad stating that he provided my mother with $250 per month in child support, which helped us meet the income requirement for the two-bedroom. The second was a letter written by my Aunt Bill declaring that my mother was the legal guardian for her son—my cousin—Kenny, who would now be living with us. With a boy child listed on the application, we now qualified for the two-bedroom apartment.

We moved, and as the two sisters expected, we never had heat, rat, or landlord problems again. In fact, we never moved again. What's more, Kenny never lived with us a single day, and I was able to have my own bedroom just like Mom wanted.

While we lived there, I got a steady job working most days after school and all day on Saturdays in the neighborhood restaurant called Brown's Fish & Chips—the one run by a friend of Mom's—located in the heart of the nearby Edenwald housing projects. I started working there when I was thirteen, before being of legal age to get my working papers, so I was paid in cash. I cooked, cleaned—you name it, I did it, including cleaning the fish and chicken that was deep fried and loved by everyone in the neighborhood.

Fridays and Saturdays were the days I worked the hardest. It seemed to be the same crowd every week that came to the restaurant—even my school friends were regular customers. The fish and chips were delicious, mind you, but that's not all they came out for. Truth be told, the restaurant was a front for an illegal bookie operation—where my mom had "hit the number"—in the days long before Lotto, Mega-Millions, and Powerball were instituted by the state.

As I think back on the setup of the place, the cash register to make your illegal bet was located in plain sight at the front of the store, less than five feet away from the second cash register where you paid for your meal. I took orders and collected payment for food but was never allowed near that other cash register. Somehow I didn't find it strange at the time; I was well aware what that register was for, but it never bothered me, nor did it worry me that I was associated with something illegal. In fact, I doubt anyone who worked or bought food there was bothered by it. I was making money to help Mom out and funding my own pocket money so she didn't have to give me cash out of her own meager wages.

No doubt our comfort level with being part of an illegal operation was helped by the fact that some of our most frequent customers were New York City police officers from the 47th precinct, located a mere three blocks down the street from the restaurant. The beat cops loved Brown's Fish & Chips, and my boss, Mr. Brown, was very friendly with the officers. Out of respect for them, he would never take a bet when they were in the restaurant. Most times, he would even give them their food without charging them. Needless to say, we never had a problem with those officers.

Mom worked during the day cooking and cleaning for elderly white folks when I was in school, and she slept in the evenings after I got home from school before she would get up and leave for her night shift at the hospital. Mom always wanted me home before she went to sleep in the evenings so she knew I was safe. On the days I didn't come home straight from school because I was working at the restaurant, she was able to sleep comfortably knowing that Mr. Brown would see me home.

Sometimes, when Mom was off from work and I didn't have to be at the restaurant, I would hang out with the neighborhood kids, but I had to stay where she could see me when she looked out the kitchen window at the street below. I always had to be in the house by the time the street lights came on, and if I was hanging with friends away from the block, I would always let my mother know before I ventured away from our street. Mom was adamant about knowing where I was at all times.

In junior high, my mother stopped dropping me off and picking me up from school, as the walk from our apartment to school was only about fifteen minutes through Edenwald. By this time, my Aunt Bill and her family had moved from the rat-infested house on Boller Avenue and now lived in the Edenwald Projects in an apartment along the route that I walked home from school.

Many of my friends in junior high school also lived in Edenwald, including my best girlfriend Stephanie, whose single mother had ten kids. Her dad only visited occasionally—just long enough to father a baby before leaving again for months on end.

Stephanie and her one older sister and eight younger brothers lived in an apartment that the city had retrofitted for them. It was actually two apartments where the walls between the two had been removed. Stephanie's apartment was just around the corner from where my aunt lived, and since we visited Auntie a lot, I sometimes got to see her when we were there.

One day after school, my friends were talking about hanging out a little before heading home. Stephanie was going with the group so I decided to tag along. They were going up to the rooftop of one of the apartment buildings to "smoke some weed and get high." I looked at my watch and thought that I had enough time to hang out a little and still get home before my mother would be expecting me.

Up on the rooftop, I took two puffs off the joint, thinking that two puffs would be all I needed to look cool. I had never smoked pot before, but I had watched my friends do it, so I knew what to do to look cool like the others.

Before I knew it, I had lost track of time and was now running late. I knew Mom would be worried so I said my goodbyes and ran like a madwoman down the stairs of the building, determined to get home before my mother started looking for me.

As I reached the ground floor and wrenched open the door, guess who was standing at the front of the building waiting for me? You got it—my mother.

SHIT! I thought. *How did she know where I was?*

When I didn't arrive home on schedule as expected, my mother had walked the entire school route looking for me, asking if anyone had seen me. Someone told her they had seen me enter that particular building, so she stood out front and waited. She was waiting there with a "switch" in her hand and was ready to use it when I came out.

A switch is what we called a flimsy tree branch used to whip bad kid's asses. Usually your parents made you go pick your own tree branch or "switch" that they then whipped you with as punishment for something you'd done wrong. My mother was standing there packing her own handpicked switch.

When I saw her, she had fury in her eyes and I knew that I was in a world of trouble. She looked at me and immediately knew I had done something I had no business doing.

My mother whipped my ass with that switch all the way back home. It seemed that we would never get to our apartment. As my friends came out behind me from the building, they immediately scattered like dust. They must have seen the wrath in my mother's eyes. All she kept saying as she practically dragged me down the street was, "Is this what you want to do with your life? Is this what I work so hard for? What the hell were you thinking? I can't believe you would do this. I thought you had more sense than this!"

Mom was so disappointed. I should have been mad at her for whippin' my ass in front of all my friends and the entire neighborhood, but I wasn't. I was sore from the lashes, but more embarrassed that my friends and neighbors saw me get a whooping and ashamed that I had let my mother down. Today, she would probably be arrested for how she whipped me in the street that day. Surely someone watching would have called Child Protective Services or the police, but it was a different time, and folks looked out for each other's kids in a different way. My guess is that they instinctively knew that my mother meant well and that I was getting what I deserved.

When we finally reached home, Mom fell exhausted into a kitchen chair. I was bruised and crying. She looked at me and asked again, "What on earth were you thinking?"

"Momma, I didn't do that much, I swear! I was just trying to be cool like my new friends."

"Your cool, new friends ain't going nowhere!" she said. "You, on the other hand, can be anything you set your mind to if you stop following them dumbass kids! You need to pick better friends, and by the way, if I ever catch you doing that shit again, you will never be able to sit down in a chair ever again! Now go and take a bath. I need to get some sleep so I can go to work tonight!"

That was it. She went into her room and I went to take that bath I sorely needed. I doubt either of us slept much that night. I remember barely being able to sit the next day, swearing to myself never to do anything to get another whippin' like that one. I knew she would live up to her promise that it would be worse the next time.

I still hung out a little after school with that crowd, but never again did I join them on the rooftop. I refused to follow someone doing anything that I knew my mother wouldn't approve of. I never wanted to disappoint her again, and my friends never questioned me when I would make excuses to leave. I think they knew my mother was a badass who would whip them too, if necessary. Her message was loud and clear that day: No child of hers would do drugs.

When my girlfriend Stephanie got pregnant later that school year, all my mother kept saying was, "See what I told you?! Is that what you want for your life?"

As Junior High School wrapped up, my friends were all looking forward to entering Evander Childs High School in the Bronx, which was rumored among the neighborhood kids as a place where weed was plentiful.

I'd usually just sit back and listen when the other kids talked about what we had to look forward to in high school. They were eager to go to Evander, but I was scared shitless. Stephanie was pregnant and would be going to a school in the city for pregnant girls. Others in my circle of friends were pregnant too, and Derrick, the boy I liked, was now a regular pothead. I wasn't having sex or doing drugs, but I was hanging out with kids who did both regularly. If I ever felt pressure to do either, my excuse was that I had to leave to get to work.

During a trip to my dad's house one weekend, I kept thinking about how much I didn't want to go to Evander. I was afraid I would eventually cave in to all the pressures to do the things that were happening all around me. When my dad took me home that Sunday, I went to my room, but I could hear him and Mom whispering in the kitchen. After a few minutes, Mom called me.

"Daddy says that you were extra quiet this weekend. Is everything okay?"

I was normally a quiet kid, but with everything going on in my head, I had been more silent than usual that weekend.

I looked at Mom and Dad and with no warning burst out in tears. "Please don't make me go there!" I said. "I don't want to go! I don't want to be like them!"

My poor parents had no idea what I was talking about and simply stared at me. My dad probably thought I was saying I didn't want to go back to Connecticut with him ever again.

Daddy then said, "Baby girl, what are you talking about? Where don't you want to go?"

"I don't want to go to that high school. I hear there's nothing but drugs there. I'm afraid to go. Please don't make me go. I don't want to be like them!"

I threw myself into my mother's arms. "Mommy, please don't make me go there. I can't. I'll do anything. Please!"

Together my parents settled me down. I think they were lost on what to do about the situation, being caught off guard as they were. In hindsight, I'd caught myself off guard too.

"But that's the school the kids in this area are assigned to attend," my mother said. "Where else could you go?"

"What about one of those private schools?" I asked. "Could I go to one of those?"

"But Val, we can't afford those schools," my mother said.

"I'll pay," I said. "I'll work and pay as much as I can. Please, Mommy? Please, Daddy?"

My eyes pleaded to both of them as they looked at each other and stared back at me. They clearly saw my fear —and determination.

"Let's look into it and see what we can do," my dad said.

That night I started looking up schools in the phone book. I already knew of one Catholic school in the area, Cardinal Spellman High School, because I walked past it every day walking to and from junior high. But I found another all-girls Catholic high school across town I hadn't heard of before named Saint Catharine's Academy. It didn't matter to me that it was foreign and not close to home. I was determined to do something different and avoid being like the friends I was hanging out with.

Both schools required an application and $250 in monthly tuition. When I presented the options to my mom and dad during his next visit, they looked at me as if I had lost my mind.

Mom said, "Val, but we aren't Catholic!"

"Please Mommy," I pleaded, "just let me apply and see if they'll take me. If I get in, I've figured out how many hours I have to work to help pay at least $100 of the tuition each month if you guys can cover the rest."

My parents agreed to let me apply. I suspect they didn't anticipate a non-Catholic to be allowed into either school, but they went along with it, no doubt without any idea of how they would cover the monthly payment. They must have thought that once I wasn't accepted, the issue would simply go away.

A few weeks later, I received acceptance letters to both schools. Cardinal Spellman, however, offered me a conditional acceptance, requiring that I attend summer school and take prerequisite courses. I couldn't do that because I had to work to start saving money for my tuition, so by process of elimination, I accepted the offer to attend Saint Catharine's.

AS PLANNED, I LEFT my junior high school friends who were headed to Evander, with no idea where the thought of leaving my friends and going to a different school came from. It hadn't even crossed my mind before the words came pouring out of my mouth that day in the kitchen with my parents.

I didn't know what I wanted to do with my life, but I sure as heck knew I didn't want to be like most of the kids I'd been hanging around with. I wanted to make my mother proud; I would pay the entire tuition if I had to. While it was a huge sacrifice for me, I was confident that I could work hard and help pay my way through high school; I was less confident that I would survive the high school pressures that would follow my friends as they entered Evander Childs High School.

"Is that what you want?" continued to echo in my mind. My mother had said those words after catching me trying pot, then again when my best girlfriend got pregnant, and they had stuck with me—so much so that I made a conscious decision not to follow the crowd, to make my own way. Their kind of life would not be mine.

9

———◆•◆———

THE OTHER SIDE OF THE TRACKS

———◆•◆———

ENTERING HIGH SCHOOL, I felt like a fish out of water. The Hillside apartments where we lived were mostly filled with low-income minority families, and the restaurant where I worked served mainly minorities who were poor and barely making ends meet. Saint Catharine's Academy couldn't have been more different. I had run away from an environment full of drugs and the pressures of urban teens, only to run right smack into a world I knew nothing about.

At home, I rarely saw white people, yet at school, there were very few blacks. The student body was ninety percent white Italians who all lived in two-parent homes their family owned. Not only was it my first time in a predominantly white environment, it was also more difficult academically than what I was used to. When I was in junior high, I got away with doing my homework between school and work. Now, I needed to stay up late to get through it.

While it was initially awkward adjusting to a new school, more demanding schoolwork, and new friends, I eventually settled in and became more comfortable in my new environment. My lifelong experience with change over the years had prepared me for adjustment once again.

Shortly after I entered high school and got my working papers, I changed jobs. Because I needed to work every day after school and as much as I could on weekends to help pay my tuition, I was thrilled to land a job as a cashier at a Key Food supermarket not far from school. I didn't have enough time to get there by bus, so Mom would pick me up from school and drop me off at work. Then she would go home, sleep some, wake up at 10:00 p.m., and drive back across town to pick me up from work, drop me off at home, and then head to work herself in time for her midnight shift at the hospital. That was when I would complete my homework for the day.

Working at the supermarket was very different from the restaurant. I didn't know anyone, nor did I recognize any of the customers, but it was a legitimate job with a real paycheck, which was all I cared about. I was really good at that job too. I had taken a typing class in junior high, so in addition to being good with money, I was also a fast typist on the register. In fact, I was the fastest, most accurate cashier on the front end during the time I worked there, for which I was very proud.

Supermarkets in those days didn't have the fancy scanner machines of today. You had to know how to add, use a real cash register, and most importantly, handle money and count change without the machine doing it for you. Having worked in the restaurant business, I was grateful for my extensive experience with money.

The area where the Key Food supermarket was located was a predominately Jewish community, which was another first experience for me. Although it's a stereotype, the customers who shopped there always seemed eager to find a bargain. The little old people loved coming through my line, loaded down with the coupons they had clipped out of the Sunday paper. In those days, we didn't have the little discount cards everyone carries around today on their keychains. If you wanted the sale, you had to work for it by going through the paper and cutting out the five- and ten-cent coupons for the items you wanted. When "double coupon days" would come around, we were even busier because the little old Jewish ladies would save up their coupons for those days to get the extra savings. I had never seen anything like it. No one used coupons at the Fish & Chips restaurant, or in any of the local bodegas in my neighborhood for that matter. But these people were determined not to waste a cent they didn't have to.

Heeding my mother's words, "Whatever you do, be the *best*," it didn't take long for me to get promoted to front-end supervisor and then eventually night book-keeper. Here I was, only in high school, and I was now closing the books for the supermarket. It goes without saying that I learned a lot from that job. I even started clipping coupons for when Mom and I would go to the grocery store. Because I'd noticed that the prices there were always cheaper than in our neighborhood, we now shopped at the supermarket where I worked. Just like the little old Jewish people who didn't seem to have much, we were now saving a little bit too.

I worked in the supermarket for two of the three years I was in high school, but by senior year, I had switched to being a part-time teller in Dollar Dry Dock Savings Bank in Co-op City in the Bronx, another heavily populated Jewish community during that time.

Again, I was in a job that suited my skills. I was always a good performer who was well liked by my regular customers—they enjoyed coming to my teller window to carry out their banking transactions. Many of the customers who became my regulars had similar charac-teristics to those who had become my regulars in the supermarket. Like those who clipped the five- and ten-cent coupons every Sunday to save every penny they could, these people also dressed very simply, often wearing the same clothes each time they came in. They didn't look like they had any money to speak of … or so I thought.

While working at the supermarket, I learned that saving every little bit helps; and while employed at the bank, I learned that looks can be deceiving. Imagine my surprise when I discovered that the same kind of people who pinched pennies in the supermarket were doing so to stash the bulk of it in their bank accounts!

Rarely did my customers come into the bank to withdraw money from their accounts. Instead, they would come in once a month to cash their checks and then deposit most of it. They would then give me their savings account passbook and ask to update their balances. They never touched their savings; they simply watched the money grow.

The same type of people—white people with worn clothes, eager for double-coupon savings—would make a regular trip once a month to bring their passbook to the window just to have their interest posted to their account. Hundreds of thousands of dollars sat idle collecting interest. I had never seen that much money in my life and definitely didn't know anyone else in my neighborhood who had that kind of cash tucked away.

I would go home and tell my mother about the hoards of money these people had stashed away and she would listen attentively and tell me, "These are good lessons you're learning that one day you'll put into practice."

Saint Catharine's turned out to be the blessing I needed to see a new world of possibilities for myself. The change in environment in school and work were eye-opening experiences for me as I got to see a different way of life: one that was unlike what my friends and I were learning in Hillside and Edenwald.

It wasn't that Saint Catharine's didn't have some of the same pressures of Evander; it certainly did. When school let out at the end of each day, for example, there was a line of boys waiting outside to pick up their girlfriends in their fancy cars. What we did on rooftops back in my neighborhood, these kids did in parked cars that their families could afford to buy for them.

The experience of seeing how these other people lived —and saved—made me curious. *How did they do it?* I often wondered. *How could they live in such nice houses?* The people back in my neighborhood knew nothing about this life—and neither would I had I not made the dramatic shift across town to Saint Catharine's Academy.

Mommy and me, circa 1965.

Aunt Babe, my "sisters" and me, circa 1969.

*Jay and Ankie, circa 1958
(cousin Lewis, who was like a brother to
us, is sitting on the porch).*

Mommy and Ankie, circa 1978.

Daddy and me, circa 1988.

Tony's and my wedding day,
18 August 1984.

IO

ANKIE

I WAS DOING WELL AND Mom was too. Things were looking up for us, and I was starting to think about going on to college.

One day, Mom and I were relaxing at home—I was in my bedroom and Mom was in hers—when the doorbell rang. I ran out to find my cousin Lewis on the doorstep. I let him in and gave him a big hug.

"Hi, kiddo," he said a bit solemnly. "Where's your Mom?"

"Mom, Lewis is here," I called out as I went back to my room.

Minutes later, I heard my mother crying, so I dashed

back out front to see what was happening. Lewis had come to break terrible news: my brother Ankie had died.

I immediately broke into tears and ran back to my room. My brother hadn't lived with us in years, but he was very special to me. No matter how busy he was or how far apart we lived, Ankie often called to check on me and ask how I was doing in school. When we visited him, he always treated me in the most special way. As a matter of fact, both my brothers doted on me when we were together. They were fiercely protective of their little sister.

When my mother came into my room a short time later, she found me crouched in the corner of my closet, shaking and crying silently. I had seen from her initial reaction to the news that she, too, was devastated, so I had crawled into the closet, not wanting her to see me cry or to upset her any more than she already was.

When she discovered me, she simply held her arms out for me to come to her. She had no words this time. We just held each other and cried.

MY BROTHER WAS TRULY a wonderful man. He was a friendly, kind, considerate person who loved to laugh and have fun, and we all loved being around him. But although he was a hard worker, he—like my mother—always seemed to struggle financially.

Both my brothers learned to be handy like my father, going on to have careers in the construction industry after the military. My brother Ankie attended technical school to become a tradesman, specializing in hanging sheetrock. My brother Jay still says that he has yet to meet anyone who hung and plastered sheetrock as perfectly as our brother Ankie did. He worked doggedly and was good at what he did, but he constantly struggled to keep money in his pocket.

Ankie and Mommy had a strong, unbreakable bond. He would call to talk to her often, and when she didn't hear from him, she would call to check on him. If he needed money, she would send what she could. So when the news of my brother's death reached her, I believe my mother's heart was permanently broken. It was as if the minute his heart stopped beating, hers was forever shattered. Like her, he was incredibly industrious and always strived to do the right thing, but he had more going on in his life than any of us realized.

My mother's instinct was to protect and save each of her children like she had done for me throughout my life. She was determined that we not fall prey to drugs. But on that day, we learned my brother had a drug problem. He hadn't died of an overdose, though. He had put a gun to his head and pulled the trigger.

Knowing my mother, I imagined she was silently blaming herself for not knowing the full extent of his struggles, for not doing more to save him. Mom stood tall amidst her heartbreak, but I don't believe she ever recovered from Ankie's suicide. Sometimes I would catch her with tears in her eyes, but she would brush them away and focus on me. Mom became even more protective of me after Ankie's death, and even more determined that I work hard and be successful. Months later, when she was still in pain over his death, she nonetheless showed no outward signs that she had lost hope. I thought she was okay because she always was.

WHEN I GRADUATED FROM high school, my mother was overcome with pride. My parents, my brother Jay, and my cousin Lewis were all at my graduation to cheer me on, going out of their way to make the day happy for me. My brother Jay kept putting his arm around my shoulder and saying, "I'm proud of you, baby girl." Lewis, who was like a brother to us, was right there smiling and hugging me too.

I cried at the memory of our brother Ankie who should have been there to cheer me on too as I crossed the stage to accept my diploma. But I knew that even though he wasn't there physically, he was with me in spirit, proud that I had successfully completed that stage of my education and was headed to Fordham University at Rose Hill in the fall. I had always wanted to return to South Carolina for college, but I decided to stay in New York and attend nearby Fordham in the Bronx to stay close to Mom, who I knew still needed me.

11

TONY

I ENTERED FORDHAM UNIVERSITY in the Fall of 1982 and almost immediately met a guy I was smitten with at a school basketball game. He was skinny, crazy tall, and incredibly handsome, and his name was Tony Rainford. His best friend Michael Cooper was a senior and star player on the Fordham basketball team. Tony was visiting Michael to see him play, but he spent more of his time staring and smiling up at me from the stands below as I cheered on the team. Fordham won that day, and we both went to the celebration on campus that followed. Once again Tony kept smiling and staring. I pretended not to notice, but I was definitely attracted to him as well.

A few days later, the phone rang. It was Tony. He and Michael had looked me up in the Fordham freshman directory and found my name and number. I was flattered that he went to all that trouble to track me down, and we talked on the phone for four hours that night. The following day, he met me after class and escorted me home from school. We were instantly inseparable.

My mother adored Tony, and my dad and brother Jay liked him as well, so we had their "approval" to date. We attended Fordham basketball games together and went dancing and to the movies. We also loved to play arcade games—especially Ms. Pacman—at the neighborhood bowling alley on Gun Hill Road in the Bronx.

But the date that will go down in history as my favorite was when Tony stopped the car in the middle of Times Square and got out to dance in the middle of the street, telling me that he loved me. He didn't care that people were honking their horns at him. Crazy in love, that's what we were. If only my mother knew that he had stopped traffic in Times Square, he would have never been able to borrow her car again.

I was only nineteen and he twenty-three when Tony asked me to marry him, but I didn't hesitate to say yes. And although our families were initially resistant, they eventually gave us their blessing. I was actually surprised Tony didn't back out of the proposal from the scrutiny he received from Jay and my father—they both made a point of making sure Tony knew that he needed to take good care of me, but it was my father who tried to make Tony run like mad in the opposite direction.

Tony and I had borrowed Mom's car to drive up to Connecticut to visit Dad, who was an avid hunter and gun collector. He stored his guns in the basement of his home and was known for making his own bullets to use when hunting deer. During that visit, Daddy invited Tony down to the basement to see a new gun he had recently purchased. After showing off his new gun, Daddy said, "Tony, have I ever showed you how to make your own bullet?"

"No, sir," Tony replied.

"Oh, well then let me show you how it's done."

Daddy instructed Tony how to load the shell with gunpowder. He had never made a bullet before, so Tony was beaming when he finished.

"Good for you son," Daddy said. "You've just made your own bullet!"

"Thanks, sir."

"Now let me explain something to you, son, about this particular bullet," Daddy went on. "This bullet that you just made, it's the bullet I plan to shoot you with if you don't take good care of my daughter. Do I make myself clear?"

Tony laughs when he tells that story today, but he wasn't laughing that day. In fact, he almost peed his pants. I knew without a doubt he loved me if he still wanted to marry me after the stunt my father pulled.

We were young but we had everyone's blessing. We got married during the summer break between my sophomore and junior year at Fordham, not wanting to wait because we couldn't bear to be apart. We had such dreams and delighted in planning every detail of our life together, but never could we have planned for the tragedy that would occur just one month after our wedding day.

12

---•◦•---

A MOTHER'S PAIN

---•◦•---

AFTER MY MOTHER DIED, I was lost and confused. I quit working and dropped out of college as I couldn't concentrate on anything. School didn't matter anymore. Nothing did. My head was filled with conflicting thoughts and my heart was too heavy with grief to make room for schoolwork.

Perhaps my heaviest burden was that nothing made sense. It seemed as if the one major belief I held while growing up—that hard work was all that mattered—was a lie. My mother was the most hardworking person I knew, yet she ripped herself out of my life with no warning or explanation.

I floated through my days in a fog but was increasingly grateful to have Tony by my side, who was there for me at every turn. My brother Jay was there for me too, but he was miles away in South Carolina, dealing with his own pain over our mother's death.

But the relationship from which I drew the greatest solace during this time was with my maternal grandmother, Corinne. Always an incredible force in our family, she continually inspired me with her resilience because her life, like my mother's, was also fraught with great sadness and struggle.

Descendants of emancipated slaves, Grandma had no formal education. She had her first child when she was sixteen and was a widow at the age of thirty. She didn't learn to read or write until she was in her sixties, in 1965, after the passage of the Voting Rights Act when blacks were required to read in order to exercise their right to vote. She would practice by reading the Bible, her favorite book.

My grandmother was a faithful servant to the Lord first and to her family second. She was a quiet woman, rarely speaking unnecessarily, but when she did, you knew to pay attention because what she had to say was important.

As a child I loved to visit her down in the countryside of Elloree, South Carolina, but by the time I moved to New York at age six, Grandma was living there as well with my Aunt Flossie, the youngest of Grandma's children. The rest of the siblings had also left home and migrated north in search of better job opportunities.

My Aunt Flossie was the only one of Grandma's children to finish high school. She went on to complete nursing school and land a position at Misericordia Hospital in the Bronx, where, as I mentioned earlier, she helped my mother get a job as a nurse's aide.

Grandma would take care of my cousin Darryl and me at night while our mothers worked the midnight shift at the hospital. It was during this time with Grandma that both Darryl and I built an incredible bond with her. Grandma was by now seventy years old and could no longer work the fields, but she was still physically strong. She loved to cook and care for us, and Darryl and I would sit and talk with her while she combed my hair at night. We would then take turns combing her long white hair and braiding it into a single plait before she went to bed. Grandma encouraged us to do well in school, saying, "I'm counting on you two to take care of me when I can no longer take care of myself."

Grandma's watching over us lasted for a little over a year before she announced to the family that she was moving back to South Carolina. After living alone as a widow for thirty-eight years, she had found love again. She and Mr. Willie Dash—a man she had known all her life—had exchanged love letters during the time she was in New York caring for us, and they planned to get married.

I recall the day that our entire family—uncles, aunts, cousins, and grandchildren—traveled down to the Port Authority in New York City to see Grandma board the Greyhound bus back to South Carolina. She was glowing with happiness. Mr. Dash had sent her the bus ticket so she could return home to become his bride. As she hugged Darryl and me together to her bosom, she reminded us that she was counting on us to finish school and be successful so we could take care of her like she took care of us. We cried all the way home, melancholy to see her go.

My grandmother and Mr. Dash were a wonderful couple, and he was the only grandfather I ever knew; my other grandparents had all passed away before I was born. Mr. Dash, like Grandma, had been widowed many years prior to their marriage to each other, and after a lifetime of being a sharecropper, he lived in a home on old Mr. George Allen's land. The Allens had built the home especially for Mr. Dash and his first wife to live in while sharecropping the surrounding fields. The first Mrs. Dash had died leaving her husband with no children of his own, and he had lived alone in that little house for years. Now, with my grandmother as his wife, he would finally have a companion to share his life with.

Grandma and Mr. Dash were faithful members of Brown Chapel African Methodist Church, the same one where my parents attended school as children. The church was founded by freed slaves and has been our spiritual home for generations. All of my known ancestors are buried in the Brown Chapel cemetery, starting with my great-grandparents—my grandmother's parents—Winnie and Sole Snider.

Mr. Dash was a senior trustee and church treasurer, and Grandma was once again one of the church matriarchs. Back home and happy, she was—perhaps for the first time in her life—married to a man who loved her unconditionally.

Having given up sharecropping, Mr. Dash worked on

the assembly line at the local peanut factory. Though well into his seventies, he would leave for work every day with the lunch box my grandmother packed for him, and when he returned each evening, he'd call out to her, "Shug, I'm home."

It warmed our hearts to see our grandma with a true gentleman. He pampered her, opened doors for her, drove her around town to do her shopping on the weekends, and held her hand walking into church. "What else do you need me to do, Shug?" he'd often ask. He cared for her like she had never been cared for before, making these, no doubt, the best years of her life.

In return, my grandmother was a consummate homemaker. She tended to the chickens while he was at work, and she picked and canned the figs and peaches from the trees he had planted around the house. Grandma was also a phenomenal cook. He'd sit on his favorite stool in their tiny kitchen where she prepared his favorite meals and say things like, "Shug, can I have a little more of that sweet tea? You sure do make the best sweet tea."

After dinner, they would head out to the front porch and sit together holding hands in their dual rocker as they watched the sun go down each evening. When my grandmother wasn't cooking, cleaning, or tending to their home, she would quilt. Every bed in her house—and in the houses of her children—has a quilt made by our grandmother. They are some of our most prized possessions.

Grandma and Mr. Dash were married for almost eighteen years when he died—within a year after my mother. Grandma was once again a widow, but at eighty-eight years of age, Mr. Dash had made sure that she lived at least eighteen of those years happy and loved.

After Mr. Dash died, the Allens gifted my grandmother the right to live in that house indefinitely—that is, until she died. We have no doubt that Mr. Dash had prearranged that gift with Mr. Allen before his death, ensuring that his "Shug" would always have a place to live. Never again would she be put out of her home, as she had when my grandfather died, with nowhere to go.

The small two-bedroom home with the wood stove in the living room would always be my grandmother's home. The elder George Allen vowed that it was built for the Dashes and would only ever be occupied by a Dash, and his descendants have kept his word for generations. No one has lived in that house since my grandmother died. It sits there now, vacant and overgrown with the pecan and fig trees surrounding it that Mr. Dash planted so many years ago. Even the chicken coop and original outhouse are still standing in the backyard.

On a recent trip to South Carolina, I visited that old house. I peered through the overgrown trees at the porch they had loved to sit on together after dinner—the same porch I would sit on when I visited Grandma after Mom died.

I LOVED TO VISIT GRANDMA. Being with her was always a reminder of what it took to survive anything life threw at you. She had come through many struggles, never complaining, preaching hard work and faith as the answer to overcoming any obstacle life sent your way. She would often say, "You can get through anything if you work hard enough AND pray hard enough."

In the years after Mom died, I'd go back to South Carolina as much as I could, often alone, to visit Grandma and stop by the church cemetery to pay my respects to Ankie and Mom, who are buried side by side. Without my mother to guide me, I desperately needed time with my grandmother to keep moving forward with my life.

During one such trip, shortly after Mom's death, we were sitting on the front porch in silence, just Grandma and me, swaying back and forth in the rocker. I adored being in her silence, staring out over the cotton fields. I was always at peace whenever I was with her; we didn't need words to communicate.

On this particular day, she said out of nowhere, "Do you really believe she did it? Maybe there's something we don't know. I don't believe it, do you?"

I just looked at her, stunned, realizing at that moment for the first time that Grandma—the rock and strength and wisdom of our family—was also hurting. I also grasped that our roles in that moment had instantly changed, that she wouldn't be the one to explain Mom's death to me. Silence passed between us for a few minutes before I gave her the only response I could without breaking down myself.

"She did it, Grandma," I said.

Upon hearing my words, tears came to her eyes and began streaming down her cheeks. It didn't make sense to either of us, and it was the first time I had ever seen my always-strong grandmother cry. I imagined that was how she cried when she was left betrayed, widowed, and evicted from her home, all those years before.

I turned to her and put my arms around her shoulders, not allowing myself to cry though I desperately wanted to. It was her time to grieve and my turn to be there for her. In that moment, I remembered all of the times Grandma said, "I'm counting on you two to take care of me when I can no longer take care of myself." She had spent her entire life tending to everyone else and being strong. Now she needed someone else to lean on, and that someone needed to be me.

Grandma was still healthy and physically strong, but her heart was broken beyond repair. Watching my grandmother cry, I began to understand what my mother must have felt three years before when my brother Ankie had committed suicide. Mom was so focused on me, I wondered if she ever took time to grieve Ankie's death. In her sorrow, she had to pretend to be strong for me and others in our family, but did she have any shoulders to lean on? Did anyone see her sorrow? I know I didn't.

I knew at that moment that I needed to clear my head, to be there for my grandmother, and not have her worry about me as my mother did.

Later that evening, Grandma and I knelt at the side of her bed as she did every night. We bent our heads and recited our prayers together before climbing into her bed.

Now I lay me down to sleep,
I pray, Dear Lord, my soul to keep.
If I should die before I wake,
I pray, Dear Lord, my soul to take.

Before Mr. Dash died, I would sleep in the front bedroom, usually with one of my cousins accompanying me. But I was too afraid to sleep in that bedroom alone now, preferring instead to sleep in Grandma's bed and feel her warmth next to me throughout the night.

Sometime during the night I felt cold. It was pitch black in the room and I couldn't see anything. I reached over for Grandma, but she wasn't there. I bolted up and called out for her but there was no answer. I grabbed the flashlight on the nightstand and clicked it on, sweeping the small light over the room. I saw nothing, so I went to search for her.

I had never walked through Grandma's house at night by myself. Once you were in bed, that's where you stayed. Even if you had to use the bathroom during the night, you never went to the one at the back of the house; instead, you used the "slop jar." As you might imagine from the sound of it, I preferred to hold off going until morning.

The bathroom in my grandmother's house was chilly that night. Indoor plumbing was a recent addition to the home and the warmth of the wood stove didn't reach that section of the house. I didn't think she would be back there since no one ever ventured there at night, especially if it was cold, but I also knew she wouldn't have left me in the house alone. My worry increased thinking about how sad she had been on the porch earlier that day, so I kept roaming through the house until I finally found her in the back of the house, slumped over the toilet bowl. It looked as if she had fallen down and was holding her head in her hands.

"Grandma, what happened?" I whispered. "Are you okay?"

She didn't answer.

I tried again, louder this time. "Grandma, please answer me."

This time I saw her move. Relieved, I knelt down beside her. Then she turned and looked at me.

"Gurl, don't ever interrupt Grandma when I'm prayin'!"

I remained quiet as she bent her head back down for a few more seconds, then she grabbed my hand so I could help her get on her feet. We walked back to her room in silence, hand in hand, then crawled into bed in our quiet ritual, me hugging her tightly. I had a hard time falling asleep this time around, but the next thing I knew, the rooster was crowing in the daylight.

Blinking awake, I saw that Grandma wasn't next to me. Though I was still a little concerned about her well-being, I knew she typically got up with the chickens, so I wasn't worried about her absence. I padded into the kitchen to find her making breakfast and humming one of her favorite gospel hymns, "What a Friend We Have in Jesus."

What a Friend we have in Jesus,
all our sins and griefs to bear!
What a privilege to carry everything to God in prayer!
O what peace we often forfeit,
O what needless pain we bear,
All because we do not carry,
everything to God in prayer.

When she saw me, she smiled. "Good morning, my girl. Are you ready for breakfast?"

"Yes, ma'am."

"Well, go brush your teeth and come sit down then. Everything's ready."

As I passed through the kitchen toward the bathroom, I kept looking for yesterday's sadness in her face, but none of it showed.

I LEARNED A LOT about my grandmother—and my mother—in that 24-hour period. As a child, Grandma was always the first one up in the house. When the rest of us would finally stumble out of bed, she was busy doing some sort of chore: feeding the chickens, collecting their eggs, or cooking so that there would be plenty of food to eat in the house. And whatever she was doing, she was always humming either a gospel tune or a Negro spiritual song.

I realized that morning with Grandma that my mother often did the same. She, too, could be found singing a hymn—some church song with words of her faith in God—while working around the house. I wondered if my mother's singing was also an antidote for her pain and suffering. How often had my mother called on God in song to ease her tired hands and broken bank account?

It came to me that both of these strong and seemingly impenetrable women had their own personal moments of weakness, and that in the darkness of night, when no one could see their pain and worry, they had likely relied on their faith in God to help them get past the pain and struggle.

LATER THAT DAY, sitting again on the front porch, rocking and staring out over the fields in silence, my grandmother simply said, "She forgot."

I knew that she was talking about my mother.

"What, Grandma? What did Mom forget?"

"She forgot what I taught her," she said, turning to me. "She forgot that the good Lord don't put no more on you than you can bear." Then, pointing and staring at me dead in the eyes, she added, "You. You must never forget." Then she rose up from the rocker and went inside.

I realized in an instant that my grandmother had probably prayed the night before for an answer to why my mother killed herself, an answer that would ease her grief and align with her unwavering faith in God. It was the only explanation that made sense to my grandmother, and as she said it, it was the only explanation that made any sense to me. My mother had gotten tired of fighting. She knew how to fight to keep going when things were rough, but for some reason she had lost her will, her hope, and her faith that tragic day. She forgot to call out to God for strength through prayer. Maybe she did but found that God had not answered in that moment. She failed to do what she had done on so many occasions before: keep going, keep pushing, and keep praying until her prayers were answered.

My grandmother's words were a reminder to me that survival takes more than hard work. When we work hard, it's because we're reaching for something. We continue to fight because we understand that there is something better coming—a light at the end of the tunnel, the hope for a brighter day. But none of it matters if you lose your faith. When the hard work doesn't seem to be making a difference, faith can keep you putting one foot in front of the other, day after day, until that brighter tomorrow shows up.

When I went back into the house, I found my grandmother humming another of her favorite gospel tunes in the kitchen.

Amazing Grace, how sweet the sound,
That saved a wretch like me
I once was lost but now am found,
Was blind, but now I see.

Grandma and I never talked about Mom's death again after that day. We had both said all that needed to be said, and from there we would move on. On that day we both accepted the fact that my mom had taken her own life and we had no idea why, so we latched on to the only explanation that made any sense: that she had lost her faith.

Like so many families, we didn't talk about the tragedies. Though the pain was always present, we tucked the sad times away in a safe place, not wanting to air our dirty laundry. Yes, we talked about her, but it was about the good and the funny times. Grandma's outward strength and positive memories of Mom helped me to think of her in the same way, and watching how Grandma dealt with the pain helped me learn how to deal with it as well. It was clear that Grandma didn't understand what happened or why and that she was heartbroken over it, but she moved on. She helped me move on as well.

Grandma would say, "Everything in life happens for a reason. You may not understand and may not be able to explain it when it happens, but keep your faith in God and He will eventually help you understand."

After that particular visit, I went back to New York and re-enrolled at Fordham. I was determined to finish my degree and make my grandmother and mother proud. It was what my mom had worked so hard for. I couldn't give up on that dream now.

I3

• ◆ • ◆ •

LETTING GO OF WHY

• ◆ • ◆ •

M Y FATHER RETIRED BACK to South Carolina in 1988, and I would see him when I visited my grandmother. Despite the fact that I mostly only saw him on weekends growing up, we had a nice relationship. He was a simple, pleasant man who rarely lost his temper—I can actually count on one hand the times I saw him lose his cool, and it was never with my mother or me. What's more, he never seemed sad. In fact, I can recall seeing my father cry only twice, when a single tear rolled down his cheek at the funerals of my brother and my mother.

My father loved to tell jokes and fun-loving stories of my brothers growing up and getting into mischief—how

Ankie was the one to get them *into* trouble and Jay was the one to get them *out*. "Ankie would pick the fight and Jay would finish it," Daddy would say, "always stepping in to defend his little brother."

After my mom died, my father made sure to stay in touch with me, and my relationship with him became stronger. He always called at 6:00 a.m. sharp on Saturday or Sunday mornings, and Jay and I would laugh and compare notes about who he'd call first each week and what funny thing he had to say to us. He would quip, "What are you doing in bed, girl? If the chickens are up, you need to be up." Or, "You can't get nothing done laying in the bed all day! What's a young girl like you doing in the bed so late? Don't you have things to do?"

"But, Daddy, it's 6:00 in the morning!" I'd say. "Some people don't wake up with the chickens."

"Well, if I'm up, you need to be up. Don't you have to go to work today?"

"No, Daddy. It's Saturday. I don't work on Saturdays. Remember?"

He clearly didn't remember because those 6:00 a.m. calls kept coming. To this day I still pop out of bed by six after so many years of receiving Daddy's early-morning phone calls. I also call or text Jay at that same hour, knowing that, like me, he developed the habit of rising early.

Our parents both dated other people while I was growing up, but to my knowledge never reconnected with each other. My mother remarried Moses, but "Thank God she had the good sense to leave him," as my grandmother would say. But my father never remarried, and if you heard the loving way in which he talked about my mother, you would think they hadn't been divorced for almost twenty years when she died. After all that time, he still referred to her as "my wife."

My father lived for seventeen years after my mother passed. During those years—first with him and my grandmother, and then with only Daddy after Grandma passed—none of us ever talked about Mom taking her own life. It was as if it was too painful to say out loud. I eventually came to understand what my grandmother and father no doubt understood: that sometimes things happen in life that we just can't explain.

SOMETIME DURING THE TEN years after my mother killed herself, I finally stopped questioning why. I no longer needed to know. I eventually accepted the reality that the explanation of "why" died with her. I came to realize that it wasn't healthy for any of my relationships for me to keep dwelling on a question that I would never know the answer to.

I also ceased blaming myself and instead began to focus on the fullness of her life—and of my brother's too—balancing the sadness with the goodness inherent in each of them. I convinced myself that that one day would not define her forever in my mind. Had I not learned to do that, I probably would have gone crazy a long time ago.

I can only imagine the countless number of people who've experienced a tragedy and spent the rest of their days on earth questioning why, blaming themselves when there was likely nothing they could do. My grandmother's simple explanation, that Mom simply forgot that "the good Lord don't put no more on you than you can bear," eventually became enough for me. I now understand, however, that that simple explanation is not actually simple at all.

AFTER MY GRANDMOTHER DIED, she continued to guide and coach me from afar. I could hear her words, sense her speaking to me regularly as if she were still here on earth with me. "Pray on it," she'd often say. And when she would come to me in a dream, it was always with warm words of encouragement.

Ironically, as I started to let go of the guilt and accept my mother's death, she too would come to me. I couldn't hear her when my mind was swirling with what-ifs and guilt, but later—once I began to let go of those emotions—I could hear her saying, "I'm sorry. I wasn't thinking. I made a mistake. Please don't hate me. I was just so tired. I should have hung in there."

But her words of encouragement came to me too. When I was doing well at work, she'd say, "Baby girl, I am so proud of you!" When I felt down or was losing confidence, she'd say, "You can do this. You can be everything I couldn't be." After a rough day at work, I'd hear, "You get up, dust yourself off, and go back in there tomorrow with your head held high. You're gonna run that damn place one day."

Even in death, my mother was a badass and still my biggest cheerleader.

THE
NEXT
CHAPTER

14

SHARING MY STORY

WHEN I RETURNED TO **Fordham University** in the Spring of 1985, six months after my mother died, I was determined to finish on time because that was what she would have wanted me to do. I doubled up on classes, took summer courses, and made up for the lost time, and Fordham allowed me to walk through graduation in June 1986 with my original classmates despite being three credits short of my degree requirement. I sat in the audience with tears rolling endlessly down my face, crestfallen that my mother wasn't there to see me achieve her dream for me. I finished the one remaining course in the fall and officially received my degree the following January.

With the help of Fordham's Career Planning and Placement office, I secured an interview on campus that resulted in a job offer and subsequent placement at the Federal Reserve Bank of New York. I entered the working world and rose quickly through the ranks, building a reputation as a hard worker with an excellent performance record. Early on, I was tapped for the Fed's elite Management Training Program, after which I moved up and around the organization, breaking records and achieving firsts. When I was thrown difficult assignments —ones that required me to pull all-nighters, sweat bullets, and cry—I remembered that my mother and grandmother often worked three jobs with little sleep and zero complaints, so who was I to complain? I was doing what my mother taught me to do and what my grandmother would remind me to do for ten years after my mother died.

What I discovered about myself as I progressed in my career was that I excelled in problem solving and crisis management—no surprise given that much of my life was one crisis after another. As a result, I built a reputation for being able to enter any challenging situation, quickly assess the issues, and devise a plan of action to resolve the problem.

Whether I was in the role of Team Leader, Project Manager, or Operations Executive, when things were in upheaval mode and many of my colleagues went into what we referred to as the "spin-cycle" (also known as blaming and explaining), I remained calm and quiet. While others spent their time dwelling on the past when faced with problems—How did we get here? What went wrong?

Who is at fault?—I typically re-directed focus to What are we trying to achieve? How do we get there? and Who can help us get there?

I essentially took a lifetime of dealing with personal challenges and new situations and turned it into a valuable skill that made me incredibly successful—without anyone's realizing where my knack for managing change and solving complex problems emanated from. No one at work ever knew my story, not because I couldn't deal with it or was ashamed, but because I simply didn't want pity. I thought that if I shared my mother's and brother's tragic end, people would feel sorry for me. Handouts and pity were not what I wanted.

When I think back on my rise in two high-profile, well-regarded organizations, I was merely doing what I was taught: work hard, push through difficult issues, and always perform with excellence. Without consciously knowing it, I was emulating my mother. The only difference between her and me was that I was fortunate to have a formal education—which I was determined to make good use of—along with the words, wisdom, work ethic, and faith taught to me by my two angels.

AS MY CAREER PROGRESSED, I became known for being a strong mentor to individuals who were trying to climb the corporate ladder or who were working through difficult circumstances, both personal and professional.

After seeing so many women who needed coaching and mentoring, Renoka—a colleague at the Federal Reserve—and I created a support group for them called

MOSAIC. Although it wasn't initially sanctioned by the company, we'd meet with the women as a group once a month over lunch and guide them in the various challenges they were facing at work and in their personal lives. We had previously experienced much of what the women were going through—the challenges of balancing personal challenges with professional growth, feeling inadequate and ill-prepared for the corporate scene, or standing out as "the only one" in the work environment. We coached them and helped them role-play difficult conversations with their bosses while boosting their confidence that they belonged there and could be successful no matter where they started or what they were currently going through. In those sessions, I would share with them some of my struggles and offer advice on how to overcome their own challenges. In exchanging these real life experiences, the women thrived knowing that if I could do it, so could they.

It was with the success of this group that I first realized the power of my story. After one year of meeting with these women, every single one of them said that the group had changed their lives and career, giving them the strength to keep pushing forward. Some of these women had changed roles from one that was not working for them to another where they felt confident and empowered; others had been promoted. All attested to having benefitted from the support, coaching, and counseling we gave them.

Through this group, I became more comfortable telling snippets of my story. I was hesitant in sharing every detail, as much of it was still too painful to say out loud, but I found a way to share enough of it to give others hope that success—despite what they were presently going through—was possible.

At that point, I began to consider giving full voice to my story. If I could make that kind of difference with corporate women, I wondered what I could do for those in the communities like the ones my mom and I had lived in. Once this spark was ignited, I was spurred on to do more. I accepted volunteer assignments working with single women and girls, and I was invited to give talks called "The Secrets of My Success" to various groups. In those settings, I began to test the waters by sharing more details of my life's tragedy and subsequent successes. When I'd say that first my brother committed suicide and then my mother did the same three years later, the reaction would be a deep collective sigh from the crowd. The pity I was so determined not to incite seemed to envelop me, yet it also felt as if the audience could feel my pain.

As I would continue speaking, I witnessed people in the audience scrunching their brows and cocking their heads to one side while looking at me, seemingly asking themselves, *How is it possible that she made it through all of that?"* I then began to give more details—of Moses, the constant moving, the different schools, experimenting with smoking pot, and the decisions I made to change my own circumstances. When I shared these parts of my past, I noticed that their eyes would open wide, not in judgment of me, but rather as if something in my story felt familiar to their own. I sensed that they felt hope that if I could do it, maybe they could too.

Over time, the crowds at my talks became bigger, and more requests came in to tell my story. The more I shared, the more I was asked to speak to groups to inspire them with how I used the struggle of my past to achieve success in my present. Lines would form at the end of my talk with participants who wanted to speak to me. Some would hug me and say how much my story inspired them to think about their lives differently. Others whispered to me that someone in their family had taken their own life as well, and they had struggled with it for years until they heard me speak about how to get past it. After receiving this feedback, I couldn't help but believe in the impact my story might have on the lives of others.

But that was only part of my healing.

Even though I was speaking publicly about my past, I still wasn't talking about my brother's or mother's deaths at home or with family. My daughters, now teenagers, were completely unaware of my family tragedies. My closest adult friends didn't know; most of my work colleagues didn't either. But my mentees and complete strangers were now finding out, and this disparity was something I was going to need to reconcile ... I just didn't know quite how or when.

15

———◆•◆———

AN UNEXPECTED GIFT

———◆•◆———

A S I GAINED COURAGE to tell my story in public, numerous people asked me if I ever thought about writing my story down on paper. While I was flattered, writing a book was the furthest thought from my mind; I was perfectly happy telling my story to small-to-medium crowds where I knew it was helping change lives.

One day over lunch, a young mentee named Ken—who also worked at the Fed—and I were sharing stories of growing up in tough circumstances. His mother had lived a hard life and ultimately died of a drug overdose after years of addiction. She had imparted a great deal of wisdom to him on her good days as he fought his own demons throughout his life, and she had made it a priority to show him that other possibilities besides a life filled with drugs existed. She didn't want him to be like her.

Ken was in the process of writing a book and he encouraged me to do the same. Though many others had encouraged me to write, Ken's words struck a different chord.

"Valerie, you've got to tell your story," he said." You're already impacting so many lives. Imagine how many people you can inspire if you tell your story more broadly. You need to make it your business to tell it while you can before someone is standing over you telling it for you! Your story will be more impactful and long-lasting if *you* tell it."

Ken's words hit me like a brick. No one else had made that point so clearly for me before. He kept talking, trying to convince me, but I didn't hear anything he said after that pointed comment. Instead, I heard my grandmother's words: "Baby girl, people come into your life for a reason. Sometimes it's not always clear when you're dealing with them, but always know there's a reason, lesson, or message that they come bearing."

I left that lunch determined to start writing, intent on changing more lives. I didn't know the first thing about writing a book, but now I was curious about doing so.

A short time later, Renoka and I were invited to participate in a conference at Spelman College in Atlanta, Georgia, to share the story of how we started and built our successful women's group, the first of its kind at the bank.

At that conference, I had the pleasure of meeting George Fraser, who was also a featured speaker and the author of the book, *Success Runs in Our Race*. I had never heard of him before that trip, but I was captivated by his message of networking and strengthening minority communities. I felt an immediate connection to his story of growing up as a poor orphan.

After George's delivery, the crowd flocked to him to get his autograph on their copy of his book. I asked for his business card but didn't join the crowd that surrounded him; I merely stood back and watched. There was something about this man and his story—and his ability to call people to action—that had my attention.

Back in my hotel room that evening, I kicked myself. *Why didn't I go up to him?* I thought. I wanted to know how one went about writing a book, and I could have asked him whether he thought my story was worth putting down on paper for a broader audience.

That night, I couldn't fall asleep. *What a missed opportunity* played over and over in my mind. But then I heard, *You have his card. Send him a note.*

I can't do that, I thought. *He probably wouldn't remember me.*

It plagued me all night until finally, near dawn, I sat at the hotel desk, drafted an email, and sent it to the address on his business card. I asked if he would have any time to meet with me as I was thinking about writing a book.

When I checked my email later that morning, I was excited to see a response. George was from Ohio but was planning an upcoming trip to New York. He agreed to meet with me for coffee when he was in town, which left me flattered yet nervous for the day of our meeting to arrive.

⚜

GEORGE AND I MET a few weeks later, and as I still wasn't clear on what I wanted to say, I simply jumped right into the conversation, giving him the highlights of my story, how I had started to tell it in small groups, and the reactions I was getting from people—namely how it was changing their lives.

I further explained that I was struggling with how to begin. I wanted to write about my mom, about navigating the corporate environment, about money management, about empowering women—the list was long, and I had no idea where to start.

George then said: "Valerie, did it ever occur to you that *this* is your life's purpose? That what happened to you occurred so that you could overcome it the way you did, and that now you can teach others to do the same? You've got a story to tell and lives to change, and you need to get to it. My gut tells me that you need to unleash the story of your mother to the world first. That will free you and provide the foundation to teach all the other things you have learned along your journey. We all need your story— to be inspired by your story. Do you know how many people out there are suffering through the same struggles as you and your mother did? They need your lessons of survival. They need your life as an example of what is achievable. Our women *especially* need to know all that is possible."

As I absorbed the impact of his words, he generously laid out tips for collecting my thoughts—guidance that became the basis for the writing of my story. After I left that lunch with George, I felt I had a roadmap, and I was filled with eagerness at the prospect of creating a book.

But despite the fact that I became more comfortable sharing my story wherever I went, that I possessed a newfound enthusiasm and confidence, and even that I believed my two heavenly angels would be proud of me for doing so, I knew I couldn't fully put my heart out into the world without first putting it out to my earthly angels ... my daughters.

16

---•◆•---

STANDING TALL

---•◆•---

I T WAS A SATURDAY, and I was at my youngest daughter Alyssa's soccer game, chatting on the field with a few other moms as we waited on the sidelines for the game to get started. The local news that day had reported a story of a man from our area who had committed suicide after losing his job, leaving his wife and two kids behind to mourn his loss.

As we discussed the story, I was consumed with the feeling that the man had lost hope. I imagined he hadn't discovered an alternative to the bad situation he was in and simply gave in to the pressure. As I reflected on what he must have been thinking—as I had done hundreds of times before when thinking about my mom—one of the women said, "He must have been deranged or mentally unstable." I froze. She said it with such authority, as if that was the only possible answer for his actions, and then the other women began to chime in, agreeing and diagnosing his mental state in great detail. They talked about his "poor" wife and kids. They remarked that they had never seen signs of him being deranged, but yet in a split second, they determined he must have been. Last week he had been a good husband, a hardworking family man, and a great dad; this week, however, as his wife and kids suffered through planning life after his suicide, he was now a closet manic-depressive.

I couldn't sit on the sidelines of the conversation any longer, so I volunteered a different perspective: "Well … maybe he just lost hope."

They all turned and looked at me as if I had two heads. "Hope?! He had everything going for him!" one woman said angrily. Another chimed in. "Yeah, a beautiful home, caring wife, and good kids." The other woman simply said, "He was a selfish bastard!"

How ironic, I thought. In their eyes, the family members were the victims and he was the deranged criminal. Yet what resonated most with *me* was the incredible pressure he must have been under. I wondered: *Were there signs of his struggle? Had he ever been in such a scenario before? Did he have anyone to confide in? Was he just tired? Maybe he was depressed and losing his job pushed him over the edge.* But whatever his circumstances, who were they to judge?

When I think about my brother who put a bullet in his head when I was sixteen, or my mom who did the same, I think about their state of mind at the moment of their actions. Both were sane people. What they had in common with each other—and probably with the man who had just taken his own life—was being overcome by the pressure and struggle with which they walked through life at times in silence. Perhaps no one was aware of the stress they felt, or that they fought hard to meet the expectations of caring for their families no matter the weight of their burden. They were good people who, in a moment that appeared to have no options for them, gave into their feeling of hopelessness.

But these women, all they could do was demoralize this dead man they barely knew. I considered walking away from their ignorant chatter, but instead I blurted out, "My brother committed suicide and he wasn't crazy!"

They all turned abruptly toward me in silence, their mouths wide open.

"And by the way," I went on, "my mother committed suicide too, and she wasn't crazy either! Did it ever occur to you that this man lived with incredible pressures to provide for his family? Perhaps he lost hope when he ran out of options to continue to do so!"

I realized that I had actually screamed those words at them, so I turned and walked to the other side of the stands. Throughout the game, I caught them occasionally glancing over at me, probably thinking I was the deranged one, but it angered me how they demonized that poor man. *Maybe his wife should have found a damn job to help him instead of hanging out with her soccer mom friends all day*, I thought. Good thing I had walked away before I said that out loud. I had somehow managed to keep that one to myself.

As I sat in the bleachers, feeling good about standing up for the man while furious with the women for their condemnation, I began to feel unsettled about what I had just done. I had never told my children of the circumstances of my mother's death, yet I had just blurted it out to a bunch of local moms.

I hadn't consciously kept it a secret; it just didn't seem appropriate to talk about, especially when my girls were small. When I spoke of her to them, I would simply say, "After my mom died ..." or "When my mom died ...." I was never questioned, so I never explained. As they got older, I knew I needed to share the details with them, but finding the right time and way to tell them was important— particularly because one of my daughters is quite sensitive and I knew it would hit her the hardest.

Knowing how small-town news would travel through the entire neighborhood by late morning, I went home after the game and devised a plan to tell my daughters. I had no idea how they would handle it, but I didn't have a choice. I couldn't let them find out from someone else.

꧁꧂

THE NEXT DAY WAS Mother's Day. I decided that sharing the story would be my gift to my girls, and I imagined my angels cheering me on. "It's about time," my grandmother said. "You have nothing to be ashamed of," my mother added.

I decided the best way to share the story was to read from the draft manuscript of the book I was in the process of writing, which not even my husband had read. Tony was supportive of my plan, but I realized I couldn't read it to my daughters without crying—and I wanted to be clear-minded to answer their questions—so I decided to print a copy for everyone, allowing the four of us to each read it together and talk about what happened as a family.

When the following morning arrived, I called everyone together and explained the gift I wanted to give them for Mother's Day. This was no longer about the soccer moms' dialogue the day before; in the hours that had passed, I now *wanted* to tell my daughters, wanted them to know the truth. I believed the incident the day before had happened to make me realize it was time.

The only guidance I gave them before passing them the book was that they had to read each chapter together and not move forward until the others had finished reading. I promised to answer any of their questions in between each chapter, and the girls were both excited. They knew that I was writing a book about my life; they just didn't know all the details.

They began by reading Chapter 1: Is That Your Mother? Alyssa kept glancing at me and frowning as she read, then when she was finished, she simply stared at me while waiting for her sister. Avaree, on the other hand, seemed captured by the story and never looked up. When they were both finished, Alyssa asked, "Mommy, is this a true story?"

"Yes," I said.

"Can we keep reading?" Alyssa asked.

"Yes, sweetheart."

By the middle of Chapter 2, Avaree needed a tissue. She said nothing, only cried. But Alyssa wanted answers. "*Why*, Mommy? Why did she do it?"

"I don't know, baby girl," was my only response.

As they proceeded to read, Avaree continued to cry. By Chapter 4, Alyssa was determined to know why while Avaree remained silent in her tears.

After a few more chapters, I asked them to stop reading so we could discuss what happened. I explained to them that for a long time I questioned everything surrounding my mother's death, but that eventually I realized I would never truly know the answer to why my mother killed herself. I shared with them that my mother had had a hard life and simply gave up one day, that I believed she felt she had run out of options and didn't know where to turn. I wanted them to understand that she didn't have a clear head that day and had made a mistake by taking her own life.

Alyssa, the analytical child, needed to understand every action, while Avaree, the sensitive child, could only cry and hug me as if she felt my pain. In many respects, my own reaction to my mother's death was a combination of the two.

A few hours later, the girls finished reading the partial manuscript. I felt a mix of emotion having fulfilled my Mother's Day gift to my children, but when each one told me she understood me even better after reading the manuscript, it was an incredible gift to me. They saw me in both my mother and my grandmother, and they now had a different viewpoint of why I always encouraged them to push through any challenge facing them.

IT TOOK ME MANY years to share my story with my daughters, but I have no regrets about not telling them sooner; I actually suspect the timing of sharing the story with my children—in their pivotal high school years when teen pressures are at their highest—may have been perfect.

While I don't tell my daughters who to be friends with, they acknowledge from my own experience why it's crucial to pick their friends wisely. They likewise understand why I constantly tell them that no one is perfect, that everyone makes mistakes, and that the key is to learn from them and to ask for help when you can't work through an issue by yourself. They also now grasp why I'm compulsive about our family finances, why I get riled when others joke about or demonize suicide, and why I can't sit through a movie that has a suicide scene. Most importantly, they understand the unquenchable passion I have to use my life to inspire others.

It also helped that I could hear my angels in the background saying, "Now, that wasn't so bad, was it?"

17

THE LITTLE BLACK GIRL
THAT COULD

NOT EVERY PARENT FEELS comfortable bringing their past out into the open with their children, and not every child will embrace a parent's—or any adult's—cautionary tale and walk a different, better path because of it. I've been fortunate thus far with my own children, but I also know from experience that hearing the story of a stranger can often have more impact than one any relative can tell. I don't exactly know why that is, but I've seen it happen numerous times when I've been asked to speak. I also know that *how* the story is delivered—especially when talking to teens—can make all the difference.

A few years ago, my good friend Arlene invited me to speak at a teen summit after hearing me tell snippets of my story during talks at corporate and non-profit professional programs. She was impressed and believed that my story should be told to teenagers, to help them realize their full potential as they deal with many of the same teen pressures I did.

The event was structured as a half-day of training around resume writing, leadership, peer pressure, and even a discussion on sexual abstinence. I was asked to kick off the program and spark their interest in the workshops to follow.

Time passed and the date of the summit approached. I hadn't given a lot of thought to how I would present my story or meet Arlene's objective of inspiring these young people beyond their current circumstances, and since I had never spoken in front of a teen crowd, I began to worry about how I would grab their attention, knowing how difficult it was to keep my own two teenage daughters focused on any one thing for long.

On the eve of the event as I was preparing my speech, I glanced over at Avaree, who was about the same age as the teens I would be addressing, and wondered if she could help me with my concerns of how to capture the teens' attention. As she sat near me watching television, I explained my dilemma of having to give a talk the following day, and of not being sure how to make it impactful for that age group.

"Mom," she said, her eyes fixed on the television, "kids in my school hate when grown-ups come in and preach to us about what we should be doing with our lives." Then she turned to me. "We get these visitors all the time who come into our school auditorium and stand up there and just *talk*. Kids don't want to hear that stuff; they want people who will encourage us. So give them examples that will make sense to them, and then they'll listen."

It was as simple as that. She resumed watching her show, and I just stared at her, pondering the wisdom of her words. I then worked the rest of the evening to craft my talk in a way that would grab the attention of the young people with whom I would be speaking, exactly like my daughter suggested.

I decided to write a story of a little girl who had suffered through incredible difficulties in her life. This story would include many examples of the struggles that the little girl faced in a way that the teens could connect with. There was so much material to write about that I didn't finish the story that night, but I wasn't worried because I had an idea for how to wrap it up, make my point, and also meet Arlene's objective of inspiring my young audience.

I formatted the manuscript into book form, and the finished product actually looked like a real book that I had borrowed for the occasion from the library. I titled it "The Little Black Girl That Could," paraphrasing the title from the well-known children's story, *The Little Engine That Could.*

I arrived early the next day while the kids were having lunch. They were your typical group of teenagers: some had come from community groups and after-school programs, and almost all were black with a few Hispanics and

Caucasians mixed in. Group counselors and a few parents accompanied them, and the kids were hanging out and having fun, much like they would in the school cafeteria.

I floated through the crowd to hear what they were talking about with each other. They had no idea—nor did they seem to care—who I was. I imagined that to them I was probably just another counselor or chaperone in the crowd checking up on them. The girls were being cute, flirting with the boys. The boys were being cool, checking out the girls. It was a Saturday morning, but somehow it felt like another typical school day for them before they rushed off to another required class.

When lunch ended, the adults shepherded the teens into the connecting auditorium-style room, and I hung back while they got organized. At this point there were still only a few adults in the room who knew who I was and why I was there. Arlene called the program to order, then walked the audience through the day's itinerary and introduced me as the keynote speaker. I meandered toward the front of the room as Arlene read my professional biography in detail, which sounded pretty impressive, even to me!

The teens gave their undivided attention as she went on to introduce me as a senior banking executive, then numerous pairs of eyes flicked my way as she continued to read. I wondered whether they were staring because they suddenly realized I was the individual who had been checking them out at lunch, or because they were surprised that such a senior person would be there to share the day with them.

Arlene shared my career accomplishments, including the fact that I had risen to be the most senior African-American woman working in the Federal Reserve Bank of New York. At that point, everyone's gaze was locked on me. As I walked to the podium, I prayed that I could keep them as engaged as they seemed in that moment.

The crowd welcomed me with applause as I stepped to the microphone and thanked Arlene. I looked into the eyes of the teens in the front rows.

"I want to start off by reading you a story that I came across, a story that will help you understand why you're here today. The title of the story is 'The Little Black Girl That Could.'" Then I looked down at my notes and began to read.

"THIS IS THE STORY of a little girl who was born to a family living in the South. She was the youngest of three children with two older brothers. The eldest brother left home to serve in the Vietnam War shortly after the little girl was born. The second brother was twelve years old when his little sister arrived. By the time he was sixteen, he and his girlfriend were having a baby of their own. They got married with the consent of their parents and gave birth to a baby boy. That brother continued to attend school, but he now had to work after school to support his new family. When he turned eighteen, he too joined the military as a way to support his family.

"In many respects, the youngest child, the little girl, lived as an only child. She doesn't remember ever living with her brothers. She did, however, become close to both of them later in life when she was a teenager.

"The parents of these three kids were sharecroppers. If you've never heard that term before, sharecroppers were typically black farmers who worked the farms of white landowners after slavery and were paid for the crops they grew. The little girl's family picked cotton and grew peanuts for the local white landowner. For their work they were paid two cents for a pound of cotton, or about two dollars a day.

"As soon as the sharecropper's children were ten years old or so, they dropped out of school to work on the farms full-time, with their parents picking cotton all day for pennies a sack to help support their families. As was common in these circumstances, the little girl's parents only went to school through the sixth grade."

I paused, looked up at my audience, and said: "Think about that. They never got to go to high school like you guys do." I had their attention so I looked down at my notes and continued reading.

"The girl's parents could read and write, but beyond that their education was limited. With little education, raising their family was hard. The parents both worked multiple jobs to keep things going. When the little girl was nearly four years old, her parents divorced, which was about the same time the girl's middle brother became a father.

"The divorce of her parents broke up the family. The father moved away and the little girl lived with her mother. It was just the two of them but not for long because the mother had difficulty finding work. She was now a single mom with a young child to support. After a period of struggle and little help from others, the mother decided to move up north to New York—where other members of her family had moved—and find work. She wanted a better life for her daughter, but that meant leaving her behind until she could get settled and send for her."

I looked up at the crowd and their eyes were locked on me, so I continued.

"The little girl stayed behind in the South, living with friends of the family. The mother of the family she was left to live with was a close friend of the little girl's mother. They were a big family, and she was well cared for, but they were not *her* family, whom she missed very much. Despite that, she lived a happy, stable life with them. Her mother sent for her in time to attend first grade, so the girl started school up north, but that didn't go too well. By that time her mother had remarried, and the little girl's stepfather was abusive. He was a nice man until he got drunk. When he drank, they would fight, and he would beat the little girl's mom."

When I looked up again at the audience, I could see they were visibly upset.

"He never hurt the little girl," I reassured them, "but the mom must not have wanted the little girl to see her be beaten anymore, so she sent her back down south."

The crowd muttered "Awww ..." at the thought of the little girl being separated from her mother again.

"For third grade, the little girl was back down south in a new school. Her mom had separated from the abusive husband and sent for her again in time for her to begin fourth grade in New York. They had their own apartment in a private house, but they realized after moving in that it was rat-infested. The little girl's mother wouldn't tolerate that, but she didn't want to send her daughter away again. So they up and moved yet again. Another apartment, another school … but at least they were together. The mother was determined not be separated from her daughter again.

"They moved a few more times until they found a place that was warm, free of rats, and that they could afford. The only problem was that the little girl would end up attending six different schools between kindergarten and sixth grade. She never had a chance to make any real friends."

I deliberately paused but didn't look up. I wanted them to think about how many friends they had sitting right there in the room with them, but how the little girl in the story had none.

"Her mom worked during the day while the girl was in school, and she worked a second job as a nurse's aide at night. The girl would take care of herself every night, all night, while her mom was at work. This started around the time she was ten years old, creating a lot of responsibility for her at such a young age.

"When she started junior high school, she finally made some friends, which made her *so* happy. Her best friend lived in a nearby building and sometimes they would go there after school and hang out. She had never had a best friend before; she had never been in one school long enough to develop true friendships and she wanted to be liked. She loved having a best friend she could confide in, but her new friends came with a lot of pressures too.

"One day, she and her best friend went to a nearby building rooftop to hang out with a few of the boys. Thank God she didn't follow all of her buddy's activities during that time because not long after she started hanging out with them, her buddy became pregnant. They were still in junior high school, and her friend was only fourteen years old.

"As high school loomed in the near future and more and more teen pressures were mounting, fear caused the girl to ask her mother if she could go to a different high school than the rest of her friends. Everyone around her seemed to be falling prey to the same pressures, and they were all slated to go to the local district high school that was well known as 'drug city.' The little girl, now a young lady, had many friends who were getting high or getting pregnant. She didn't want to be like them.

"All of the other schools in the area were private ones that neither of her parents could afford to send her to because of the tuition costs. But the girl asked if she could apply to those schools and promised that if she was accepted, she would work to help pay the monthly tuition. Her parents reluctantly agreed, not expecting her to get in. But she did. She was accepted into an all-girls Catholic school across town, and shortly after, she found a job and started working just as she promised.

"Her high school was a very different place. Uniforms, nuns, and religion class—and she wasn't even Catholic. It was scary at first, but she just kept reminding herself that staying with her friends would have been much, much scarier. She traveled across town every day to attend school. Her friends didn't understand why she had made this choice, and most of the neighborhood kids stopped speaking to her, calling her names like 'stuck up' and 'miss goodie two shoes.' They didn't want to be around her anymore. It was hard, but luckily she had school and work to fill her days.

"Her job was near her school and she worked every day until night to help pay her tuition. Her mom would pick her up from school and drop her off at work to make sure she arrived on time. She typically worked until 10:00 p.m. during the week and also on Saturdays. Then her mom would pick her up at night after work, drop her off at home, and then head to her own job at the hospital to work the night shift. The girl never had time for homework, yet despite that, her grades in school were good. She did the best she could because anything was better than what her old friends were experiencing back at the neighborhood high school.

"As time moved on, she got used to the new school and the difficult schedule while managing her schoolwork. Things were feeling stable until one day the news came that her brother, the middle one—the one who got married at sixteen to be an honorable father and joined the military to provide for his family—had committed suicide. The little girl's heart was broken. She had looked up to her brother and knew how hard he had tried to do the right thing. Her mother was distraught."

I paused and looked into the crowd. They were sitting on the edge of their seats fully engaged with the story, seeming to feel the little girl's pain.

"Things were never ... ever ... the same," I continued. "Time passed and a few years later, the young girl's mother committed suicide too."

At that point, gasps of "Oh my God" floated toward me. I then looked into their eyes, and after an extended pause said, "Rather than me read any more, why don't you guys tell me what *you* think happened to the little girl after her mother committed suicide."

They erupted in chatter with each other, visibly upset for the girl, debating her fate. I heard them trying to figure out whether she killed herself or whether she gave into drugs. They couldn't decide. I merely observed from behind the podium, fascinated with how deeply they connected with the story.

I had purposely left out some of the details of the little girl's story to keep their attention, but while I was preparing it, I had no idea what their reaction would be. Now, however, I admit I wasn't surprised by how they were questioning the girl's fate.

After a few minutes, I raised the big question.

"Okay, by a show of hands, how many of you think the little girl killed herself?"

Almost every hand in the room went up. Those who disagreed began to speak up. "No, she didn't," they said, igniting more discussion amongst themselves as they contemplated what happened.

"Okay," I said. "How many of you think the girl is alive, but turned to drugs or is an unwed mom with a houseful of babies?"

Many hands went up and more chatter began. They

were upset because they knew that something terrible must have happened to the girl, but they were in disagreement about what it was. The discussion continued as I stood there watching them. Their reaction, of course, was typical—the media had taught them that only bad things follow a life of struggle. Negative outcomes were all they could imagine since, more than likely, that was all they had experienced. Their expectations mirrored what they had seen and been taught. They weren't even considering that anything good could have happened to the girl.

Finally, I took back control of my audience.

"Okay guys. Let me have your attention. Let's talk about it together. The girl has had a terrible life, right?"

Comments of agreement came from the group.

As I reopened the book, I purposely looked down, pretending that there were more words written on the page. "Okay," I said. "Let me ask you just one more question before I continue reading so that we can find out what happened to the girl."

They were all silent, their eyes fixed on me.

"Tell me, why do you guys think I'm here?"

I looked into their eyes, but all I received were blank stares. They were clearly confused, having no idea why I had been invited to speak to them. I glanced at the adults lining the back wall of the room, some of whom began to smile.

I looked back into the questioning eyes of my teen audience and said, "I'm here because *I* am the little girl."

Gasps and stares followed my declaration. I then

stepped away from the podium, leaving the book behind, and walked out into the crowd. I wanted them to know that I was real, that I knew what they were going through. I wanted them to know that no matter the difficult circumstances life dealt them, they could overcome them with a determination to be different, that their lives didn't have to follow a negative path, that they didn't need to believe or model everything they saw on TV ... that they didn't have to be another statistic within our urban communities.

I RECEIVED VERY FEW questions from my audience that day. After the program ended, many of them simply stared at me as they left the room and headed to their workshop classes. They were clearly shocked by the twist in the story, like a surprise in a movie where you think you know what's going to happen, but something sidelines you. After the lives they'd led up to that point, they simply couldn't fathom a positive end to the little girl's story.

As I prepared to leave, the adults thanked me for sharing my story. I was pleased to hear they thought the presentation was impactful, but I was more interested in what the kids thought. I could tell they had been engaged, but I couldn't help but wonder if they would merely go home and resume their pressure-filled lives.

As I watched them walk out of the auditorium that day, I knew I had left them thinking about a lot of things, but I didn't know if any of them would do anything differently in their lives or seek new opportunities for themselves as a result. It left me wishing I had made a way to keep in touch with them to know how many were impacted in a positive way. Instead, I had to resign myself to the fact that I would likely never know.

EPILOGUE

ONE YEAR AFTER THAT teen summit, I was
invited to speak at the Harlem YMCA's 40th
anniversary awards dinner. As a long-time
supporter of the organization, the president and CEO of
our company was asked to address the audience but was
not available to attend. They had honored me the prior
year at the same event as a Black Achiever, so I was invited
in his stead to speak to the more than 1,000 people who
would attend.

I addressed the crowd just before dinner with an
intermission following my speech. As I left the stage, a
woman came rushing over to me holding the hand of a
young man dressed in a suit and tie.

"I just had to meet you," she beamed, putting her arm
around the boy. "My son hasn't stopped talking about you

since he attended a workshop last year where you presented to his teen group. He came home saying, 'Mom, if that woman can get past all that happened to her, what can I do?' Your story made quite an impression on my son. He's more focused on his schoolwork now, and I just wanted to say thank you."

I was shocked, yet excited. Never did I expect to learn about the fate of one of my teen protégés at this completely unrelated event. Beyond congratulating the young man and thanking his mother for seeking me out, I was otherwise speechless. We chatted for a bit and then went our separate ways. Only after the event did the impact of what happened hit me. Again, as on the day of that teen summit, I wished I had gotten his contact information to stay in touch.

Although I may never know how that young man's life has played out since, that one encounter was enough for me to become more deliberate about sharing my story. I already knew it was an inspiration to folks in the community and to my mentees at work, but now I had validation in the power of my story to change the lives of young people, to show them the world of possibilities that existed for them with hard work, focus, a determination to be different—and, of course, faith.

⬦

SOME TIME LATER, I received an email from another mother. She explained that she was one of the parent chaperones at the teen summit with her son on that day when I gave the "The Little Black Girl That Could" talk.

She had kept the business card I gave her and had just found it in an old pocketbook. I called her after receiving her email, touched that she had reached out to me.

She wanted me to know that her son had just graduated from Morehouse College, class of 2012, where President Barack Obama gave the commencement address. It was important to her that I know that not only did I make a difference in her son's life, but that she, too, had finished nursing school and was thriving, in large part because she had been touched by my story that day.

Once again, I was thrilled to know that my story was one of hope and inspiration to others. I told her about the book I was writing and she encouraged me to continue, convinced that many more needed to hear it. This time, I made sure we could keep in touch and have ever since.

With the passing of time, I understood it was no accident that these individuals were finding me to validate the power of my story. They were placed in my path, as my grandmother would say, to bring me a message, and I felt that message was to finally finish the book so I could inspire the world to believe that brighter tomorrows lie ahead.

༒

MY HEART SWELLS WHEN I think of these two boys out of that group of 150 teens, knowing at least two lives were changed after hearing my story that day. And while I often wonder how many more of those young people left more focused on their future and determined to be different, what I do know is that we each have the opportunity to change a life every day, to share wisdom from experiences that can help one another, even if we don't get to hear the triumphant follow-up story. What counts is what we give to lift others up around us, no matter how big or small our gift may be. Whether you're a teacher who gives your heart to your classroom every day, or a coach who guides and inspires ... a leader who brings out the best in those around you to help them develop and grow, or a blue-collar worker who sets an example of hard work and ethics to your coworkers ... an entrepreneur who uses your gifts of innovation and creativity to help others fulfill a goal or dream, or a parent who's raising loving, compassionate children ... a professional who helps others heal, or a regular ol' honest employee who's doing your best on the job and for your family ... you have the opportunity to make a difference, even if a smile is all you have to give in the moment.

Not only was George right—that I do have a story to tell—but I've been blessed to meet many more people whose lives were changed because of my story. I may not have been able to save my mother, but I have since saved others who needed a dose of hope ... and that's what I plan to keep doing.

Being honored by the Harlem YMCA.

(left)
Lewis, me,
and Jay.

(below)
Aunt
Flossie,
me, and
Aunt Bill.

Tony and me
today.

My earthly angels, my daughters,
Avaree and Alyssa.

My heavenly angels,
my grandmother, Corinne,
and my mother, Betty,
cheering us all on.

AUTHOR'S NOTE

Nothing fulfills me more than knowing I had a part in
changing a life, in improving someone's outlook.

If my story touched you in some way,
please send me a note at:

info@valerierainford.com

I would sincerely love to hear from you.

Here's hoping you achieve your brighter tomorrow …

QUESTIONS & TOPICS
FOR DISCUSSION

————◆•◆————

1. How did Valerie's story affect you? Could you feel her journey as she wanted her readers to?

2. What was the most impactful chapter for you personally?

3. In what ways did you relate to Valerie and her story? Have you had similar adversity to overcome?

4. Do you know anyone who grew up in similar circumstances to Valerie's? Did he/she succumb to those circumstances or supersede them as Valerie did?

5. What was your reaction to Betty's marriage to Moses? Were you surprised she left him? How do you think that decision affected young Valerie's opinion of her mother?

6. Do you know anyone who committed suicide? What was the impact on his/her loved ones? What are your thoughts on the topic of "loss of hope"?

7. Do you know anyone who is blaming themselves for the loss of a loved one to suicide? What would you say to them after reading Valerie's book?

8. Why do you think Valerie's mindset was so different from that of her friends, despite living in the same impoverished environment?

9. Valerie shielded her family heartache for many years. Do you believe in forming the support groups with women, she unwittingly formed a support group for herself?

10. What was your opinion of how Valerie delivered her talk at the teen summit? Do you think her choice to tell a third-person story had greater impact than a first-person version?

11. Did you find Valerie's story to be universal? Do you think it transcends race, gender, and environment to speak to a broad audience?

12. Although Valerie is a strong, driven person, do you think she would have had the courage to write her story had she not received encouragement from others to do so? Why or why not?

13. What do you think parents and educators can do to inspire more young people in similar circumstances to strive for a better life?

14. Did Valerie's story shift your thinking about how to deal with challenge and adversity?

15. Why do you think Valerie's inspiring story of hope, tenacity, and faith will change some lives for the better and not others?

VALERIE RAINFORD is the youngest child of southern sharecroppers who believes that everything that occurred in her life was intended to test her will and resilience and to prove that success can be achieved no matter where you start or what you may currently be going through. After enduring a series of trying circumstances in her young life, including the suicides of her brother and mother, Valerie stayed true to the strong ethics passed down to her from her parents and grandparents, determined to beat the odds.

After graduating from Fordham University with a Bachelor of Arts degree in Economics, she was appointed as an officer at the Federal Reserve Bank of New York at the age of 29—the youngest ever at that time in the Fed's history. By the age of 35, she was promoted to Senior Vice President, becoming the most senior African-American woman in the company's history; at 42, she was recruited by JPMorgan Chase to bring her well-regarded problem-solving skills to the private sector.

Valerie is currently a senior executive with one of the world's largest financial services firms, as well as a freelance writer, speaker, coach, and mentor who uses her work to inspire others to see past their current circumstances, whether in the workplace or in their personal lives, to reach their full potential and live their brighter tomorrow.

Valerie was honored in 2007 by *Network Journal* magazine as one of "25 Influential Black Women in Business" and in 2009 by the Harlem YMCA as a "Black Achiever in Industry." She has appeared on TV shows such as *Black Enterprise Business Report* and *Brooklyn Savvy*, and has been featured in multiple publications including *Black Enterprise* magazine and the Adecco Group's "Leadership Tribute to Women." She resides in New York with her beloved husband and two daughters.

Connect with Valerie at:
www.valerierainford.com
info@valerierainford.com